Dr. Reinhard K. Sprenger is the author of the best-selling *Mythos Motivation* (Campus, 16th edition, 1999) and independent consultant for personnel development and management training. He has advised Coca-Cola, 3M, BASF, Philip Morris, Hewlett Packard, Thyssen Handelsunion, apetito, Siemens, Fresenius, Daimler-Benz and many others. Dr. Sprenger is an associate lecturer at the universities in Berlin, Bochum, Essen and Cologne.

Reinhard K. Sprenger

The Principle of Responsibility

Pathways towards Motivation

Translated by W. J. Hadfield-Burkardt

Campus Verlag
Frankfurt/New York

Die Deutsche Bibliothek – CIP-Einheitsaufnahme

Ein Titeldatensatz für diese Publikation ist bei
Der Deutschen Bibliothek erhältlich.
ISBN 3-593-36403-4

Cover design: Guido Klütsch, Köln
Type-setting: Leingärtner, Nabburg
Printing and binding: Druckhaus Beltz, Hemsbach
Printed on acid-free paper an chlorine-free bleached paper.
Printed in Germany

People always blame circumstances for what they are. I do not believe in circumstances. Those who make a mark on this world set out to find the circumstances they are looking for, and if they cannot find them, they create them, themselves.

George Bernard Shaw

Contents

Introduction

A cost-benefit analysis

»One day I was walking through the customer parking lot of one of our department stores when I saw a gardener raking up leaves. He was using a rake which only had about 15 teeth left – normally it would have had twice that number. I asked him: ›Why are you using this old rake? You are hardly making any progress.‹ – ›They gave me this rake‹, the gardener calmly answered. ›Why didn't you take a better rake?‹ I insisted. ›That's not my job,‹ he replied. I thought: ›How can anyone give an employee such a poor quality tool to do a job? I'm going to find out who his supervisor is and have a talk with him. His job is to make sure that his people have the right tools.‹«

James Belasco told this story which illustrates in part what I am writing against in this book: the Pontius Pilatus attitude expressed primarily by »I am not responsible.« as well as an excessively exaggerated concept of leadership. This leads to questions such as: What are employees responsible for? Does giving the supervisor the responsibility solve the problem? What steps can be taken fundamentally to improve this situation? Do not all employees have to stand up for how they perform their work? And if that is true, what is the role of management? And what does it mean to »delegate responsibility?«

After I had published »Mythos Motivation« (The Myth of Motivation) I was asked – more frequently than I expected – whether I wanted to follow up this book with another. In particular many readers wanted to see a concrete »What is the better alternative?« This book is a follow-up to »The Myth« – but is in fact its forerunner. This volume does develop some of the ideas presented in the earlier book, specifically expanding on the outlined theses (especially those on the final pages) regarding self-motivation. But it does so in a way that is complete in itself. The supposed demarcation line between professional and private life – which is a misleading division anyway – is completely ignored. In any case I hope that many of you will see your own lives in this book and find your own questions answered.

The central question

I have stopped reading any books which start with »Everything is becoming more complex, faster, and more chaotic.« There are no advances worth mentioning to be achieved from the salto mortale into the comic opera world of management methods. Of course the winds have gotten a bit stiffer. Of course high-tech in the Far East and low-pay in the Eastern Europe have stiffened competition. But the basic problems in our organizations have not changed a bit. The national economist Werner Sombart formulated the central question of this book back in 1913:

»*How is this possible: that healthy and largely admirable people with above average talents can want to perform a commercial activity, not only as a duty, not only as a necessary evil, but rather because they enjoy it, because they devote their hearts and minds, their bodies and souls to it?*«

Today managers ask similarly:

- What can I do to insure that employees assume more responsibility?

- How can I harness the potential of my employees?
- How can I create a company into which employees like to come in the morning?

I would like to respond to these questions.

Questions of perspective

The mobilization of employee potential as a decisive factor for success has been well-known for years. Germany is not rich in natural resources. Our most important natural resource is people's readiness to cooperate. But, sadly, the work place frequently remains an area where initiative is absent. We run machines to full capacity, but we do not use the full capacities of people. So labor costs and structural problems are not the only things which sap the strength of the German economy. We do not utilize people to their full potential.

Most importantly, we do not vigorously require employees to assume responsibility. Many employees have dropped out, after years of being underrated, have forgotten how to assume responsibility for themselves, their motivation and their performance. Careful scrutiny reveals that large segments of the labor force are on a kind of psychological strike against the insult of permanently being expected to do work below their abilities. Their unemployment is internal. In their minds as well: work to rule.

The crisis of work is frequently still met with the old recipes which at best reflect no more than tinkering and fail to break loose from outmoded thinking. Some think they can motivate others with cash, for example, by reactivating the policy of offering monetary rewards for employee suggestions. A problem which cannot be solved by reaching for the wallet cannot be solved. But such ideas are like so much dead wood over which their employees trip.

Others think about restructuring the organization. The management mantra in this case is: open spaces, flat hierarchies, debureaucratizing, decentralizing. This second approach seems to me necessary and promising; there are quite a few notable suggestions and encouraging examples.

Still: lean management, partially autonomous work groups, kaizen, reengineering – all these management concepts can only work if people's attitudes change. The research manager Sigmar Klose at Boehringer Mannheim says: With the best structure I can achieve 20 percent. The rest is mental attitude, the will to succeed, the feeling of »We can do it!« The structural optimizers make the same mistake as each one of us who hoped that a trip to a faraway country would make us happier: Your self is always with you.

»Games are won mentally.« The tighter the field, the hotter the competition, the more important the mental attitude is with which the employees work, the management leads and sales personnel go out to call on their customers. Especially regarding attitudes towards *changes*. Thus, it is also a question of attitude whether a company – unsuccessfully – wants to remain stable in the midst of change or seeks stability in change. It is notable to see how much difficulty many employees have in seeing anything positive in change: »That won't work!« (instead of »That won't work *that way*«). »I can't do that!« (instead of »I can't do that *yet*«). Evidently the only creature which loves change is a wet baby.

So in this book I am primarily concerned with the consciousness of people on the job. With a particular manner of observing life in the company. I am concerned with involvement, initiative and the feeling of being on course in one's own journey through life. My focal point is the individual.

The sections of the book

There is no business design task more important than the re-introduction of responsibility into the company. This is even more true since there is a tendency towards fewer and fewer managers and larger and larger management areas.

As a negative foil I describe in the first part of this book the disputes within companies over responsibility, assigning blame and rationalizing. The result is: organized irresponsibility. Near the end of this part I distinguish between responsibility, what is known as individual responsibility in German companies, and commitment.

The *Philosophical Section* lays the intellectual foundation for individual responsibility, motivation and commitment. At this point I am not speaking to the manager »as manager« but to all individuals, regardless of their rank in the hierarchy. You will only be able to profit from reading this part if you are prepared to apply it to yourself, if you use it as an incentive for self-criticism. The three pillars of individual responsibility: choice (autonomy) – will (initiative) – response (creativity) are developed.

Although the subtitle of this section conjures up an image of frozen high-brow thinking, some of the perspectives brought forward there are overwhelmingly simple. The fact that they must be reiterated aptly reflects the present state of our business community. If I crusade against the non-observance of discipline, will and commitment I am, however, exposing myself to the danger that, in this context, many hide their own lack of courage by accusing others of being unrealistic in their thinking. Utopian! Theory! Or the worst of all invectives: Philosophy!

So, I'm warning you: A few passages in this first main section may well strike you as being exceptionally irritating. I would have cut them out if they had been expendable for the argument as a whole. They are not. On the contrary: These parts in particular present readers with their most serious challenge. They require the whole reader, those who are prepared to re-examine themselves and their customary ways of thinking. So I can merely appeal to you to resist the urge to prematurely put down the book. Many things will become apparent and will be explained later in the book – and I hope – in an encouraging and liberating way.

The *Pragmatic Section* illustrates the three basic principles and daily situations in management practice. The question to be examined is: What can management do to promote commitment? I contrast the widely heard call for managers to act as role models with a change in the overall approach. In the thicket of false alternatives: vision, role model, supervisor, the outlines of a forward-looking management culture can be made out.

This outline is forward looking in the sense that I bring the subjective constructivism for management questions down to earth: How are judgements about employees made? How can I change unsatisfactory conditions without undermining motivation? In addition, I discuss in relation to daily situations the possibility of employees assuming responsibility – but provide at the same time evidence that it is impossible to »transfer« responsibility, to »empower« employees. I develop the thesis that criticism does not work, and offer alternative procedures. The commitment mechanics for target agreements are described. The conclusion is provided by an essay about credibility traps.

The difference between the two main sections is also reflected by the fact that they are argued at different levels. That can be easily shown by the core question of the Pragmatic Section:

How can we create a company in which responsibility is no longer felt to be a burden but is desired?

»That is not the question at all«, is the response heard from opponents. »People want to bear responsibility; only suspicious and control-obsessed bosses stand in the way of them assuming this responsibility.« Granted. So we must open our eyes to a broader question: »What kind of management is needed to ensure employees take responsibility?« »Hold on a minute!« the other side exclaims. »The really interesting question is in fact: Why do employees pass the buck? Why do they *allow* themselves to be deprived of responsibility?«

So what I want to describe in this book is the meaning of commitment within companies and how managers can promote it. The opponents who I am pointing my finger at like the baptizer in Grünewald's painting, are the ethics of keeping your hands clean by doing nothing as well as an excessively exaggerated concept of leadership. In the latter case I would like neither to deliver a sermon nor bring unwarranted charges against managers, as has become fashionable today in most quarters. But perhaps some managers may do something which their exercising of authority frequently does not allow them to do: take time to think.

Practice

I am practical. Of course I am interested in whether an idea is cohesive but more important to me is whether it works. For the following considerations, therefore, I introduce a criterion which I call »practical«. I ask: »Is this way of thinking practical?« I do not ask whether any of the arguments and ideas are »right« but rather whether it is »useful« to accept such ideas.

So the criterion test admittedly has been chosen only on a functional basis. I move on to the substance, when I turn to the question: »Does an idea strengthen my commitment? Or does it weaken it?« To me, arguments which strengthen my commitment are, *in this regard* »true«. Ideas which are obstacles to acting, justify inaction or maintain a position of non-responsibility to me are *in this regard* »false«. As a consequence, my point of departure is a commitment to a pragmatic legitimization whose moral core is the responsibility of the individual.

So I am not speaking the truth here. If someone could speak the truth they would have spoken it already and we would not have to continue talking about it. I would like to develop positions which are practical in the sense of commitment and a responsible corporate culture. Like all ideas relating to perspective, the concepts suggested here are based on the responsibility of the individuals who must decide for themselves what they consider to be true.

However, those who feel their own ideas confirmed after reading the book – and most people want to have their own thinking confirmed by books – will not have gained much. Those who do not share my opinions at all have an opportunity to gain much more. Along with Max Frisch, I hope that »the reader will discover primarily the wealth of his own thoughts.«

Yes, there is one more thing to say – for those who have dedicated themselves to an optimistic approach to their work. Karl Popper said: »There is nothing more irresponsible than pessimism.«

Power is in the hands of the doers.

Thinking like this is simply practical.

Organized irresponsibility

In corporations the cup of responsibility is an itinerant trophy.

Ralph Stayer, Chairman of Johnsonville Foods, has had some bad experiences: »We were the sole supplier of a large customer. The customer was continuously threatening to call a second supplier because he was afraid to trust our ability to supply. ›Don't worry,‹ I assured him over and over again, ›we will always deliver on time.‹ One day we received the urgent order to modify the standard version of a product as a rush job and deliver it without fail on the following day. Our people mobilized all our available resources and actually finished on time. They packed the product and, as usual, instructed the carrier to make the delivery. Due to technical problems, the truckdriver did not turn up until the next day, and the delivery was accordingly delayed. Since then we have no longer been the sole supplier. Our employees' excuse: »We cannot monitor the truck driver. He does not work for our company. We did our job. There was nothing more we could do.«

The break for the fire escape

In companies the victim mentality is spreading. Hardly anyone assumes full responsibility for what they do. The continuous whining of the shirker articulates the stubborn will to be powerless: What can I do? The words say: »*They* don't allow it.« – »*The others* are causing the problem.« – »If *they* didn't act so stupidly everything would work out perfectly all right.« – »The Board does not provide any clear instructions!« If the Board then meets the pressing expectations, people moan about the instructions. If the competitor has been awarded the contract: »The customer didn't thoroughly understand everything our product can do.« If the employee does not do what others expect (and on top of that is still enthusiastic): »Unmotivated low performer!« – »It is not what *I* want, it is what the boss wants!« – The »front office« is responsible. The »shop floor« is responsible! The group leader is responsible for the friendliness and efficiency of employees serving customers! The quality manager is responsible for quality (what else?)! The human resources guy for the personnel! The payment system is to blame! »We« would be very successful if »they« wouldn't stand in the way. »But our company is just too big!« – »But our company is just too small!« And today we have the low pressure system coming down from the mountains which makes everyone feel weak and, besides, it's Tuesday.

There are companies which are nothing but victim clubs. You hear nothing but whining from morning to evening. About Frosty the snowman in the executive offices, about the uncooperative department next door, about employees with no initiative, about the flatterer in the neck-tie bunker, about the jerks working at the machines, about the residue-free money incinerators in the executive offices, about the customers who do nothing but disrupt work anyway. In a Berlin warehouse the walkway between two administrative areas is called the »Bridge of Sighs«. And according to one legend, the two corporate founders, Hewlett and Packard, introduced the open plan offices so characteristic of that company only because they knew that for many of their employees every office wall is a wailing wall.

If you could judge the nature of the employees based on the company's situation you would have to define people as creatures who would do anything to duck responsibility. Dr. Kimble is everywhere. In Germany the thunder of the approaching whinge-front has also colonized an additional storm center in the east: »Now I have to show initiative every day, after they had been telling me for 40 years: If you stick your neck out in our plant you'll get into trouble.« Some people idealize the past here, without having to be afraid that it will return.

Responsibility: the itinerant trophy

Fundamentally, the definition of responsibility in companies has been largely left vague. Responsibility does the rounds and swings back and forth correspondingly. Sometimes it ends up with the employees, sometimes with the boss, sometimes in the head office, sometimes with other guys, sometimes everyone is involved.

This insecurity is reflected in the behavior of all the participants: They all alternate between accusation and pity, between concern and irritated demand, between indignation and guilty conscience. The areas of responsibility get confused, it is unclear who is *really* responsible for what, everyone has a word to say about everything, management takes its disruption mission extremely seriously, there is hardly a pot they aren't constantly tending, poking their nose into and wildly stirring, wherever you look – justified? Unjustified?

This snarl of issues becomes obvious from the topics which boards of directors deal with. The misfortune of top managers is not that they are too far from the people but that they are not far enough away. It is hard to believe how many Boards of Directors are still personally involved in unimportant details: like walking through the premises after office hours with an enormous bunch of keys, turning out lights; checking to see if the number of potted plants in the offices of the department heads corresponds to the guidelines; discussion whether the seminar should be held in hotel X or Y. What's more: »I cannot shake the feeling that, besides me, nobody else does any work around here.« I heard of one director who took part in a one hour discussion on how often urinals in the plant flush. Good examples of Liza Minelli's thesis that life is a cabaret.

But what is not so hilarious is the fact that for long term consequences, less and less responsibility is being assumed. The remote-control domination of capital markets looking for short term results leads companies to operate on the basis of quick-reaction policies which are blind to their side effects or the consequences further down the road. After me the deluge! The cultivated cynicism of the shareholder value fetishists undermines every stable relationship, any idea of a company capable of long term commitment. Who still remembers Walther Rathenau, member of the AEG Board of Directors and later German Foreign Minister who developed a »principle of inner responsibility« for companies, emancipating them from profit maximizing and the goals of the share holders and had it made part of the corporate income tax law?

In addition, hardly a manager in our companies has enough leeway and time to be solely responsible for his or her era. Furthermore, as managers, due to more frequent transfers, do not even remain long enough in their positions to see the results of their decisions, there is frequently no direct responsibility for results. At Lever Europe in 1993 just under 42 percent of all the managers were on the job for less than 12 months. Managers who expect such a short stay in one office are hardly interested in long-term solutions to problems. They do not make any lasting commitment to their task or to their employees. The employees know this as well and do not commit themselves either: »We'll survive this one, too.«

This situation in our companies can be best paraphrased by an expression which Ulrich Beck coined in another context: organized irresponsibility. In divided departments, servile subordinates serve, paper pushers push paper, under the supervision of superiorly placed supervisors.

Let us take a closer look at some of these structures.

Not my responsibility!

Thomas Schalberger, PR manager from Düsseldorf, is really in a rush this time. It is ten minutes to twelve by the station clock in the hall of the main railway station in Cologne, Germany, and he is very short on time to his next appointment. He approaches the woman at the ticket counter and says, »A second class ticket to Düsseldorf.« The response is, »On an Intercity or an express?« »I don't know, whichever train is next,« says Schalberger, »you can look it up, can't you?« »I'm not the information desk,« the woman at the tick counter replies curtly, the only employees who are allowed to provide information are at the information desk. A short unpleasant exchange brings no results. Schalberger has to take his place in the line in front of the information desk – and misses his train (Spiegel 26/1994).

This scene is a compact illustration of the »Not responsible!« attitude. This is the mentality of people holding clearly defined posts, permanent jobs and positions. For this sort of mentality the question is: »Who is responsible?« (Instead of: »Who can do it best?«) Its essence is static, an identity formed by negative exclusion. It's logical location is the »work place«, a place which someone »occupies« by »filling« it and executing a sharply delineated circle of activities. Performed as they always were and as they always will be. Fragmented individual tasks provide the orientation. That's why there are job descriptions. For protective reasons, against unfriendly takeovers. They describe a territory which must be defended, and whose boundaries are not crossed on one's own initiative either. A department head who was hired in from outside by Versorgungs- und Verkehrsgesellschaft MVV in Mannheim, Germany, remembers: »The first words I learned were »competence status«, »biography« and »That is not in my job description.«

The concept »work place« corresponds on the action level to the »file«. And the file-oriented procedure of administration, in turn, rigidifies the domination of the office. Professional knowledge becomes functional knowledge and functional knowledge becomes knowledge about official channels (Dirk Baecker). At one German regional bank all new employees receive a list of people who they must *not* call.

It is easy to see that the division of labor and the organizational fragmentation of work have both played significance roles in this situation. They have turned companies into vertical hierarchies in whose functional silos areas of authority and occupational demarcation flourish. The cutting up of work processes into the smallest steps, the separation of preliminary and final activities (design, job engineering, production, final inspection etc.), which separates the workers from the office staff, the division made between thinking and hands-on activity, the higher value placed on leading as opposed to carrying out – all the items which were invented under the label Taylorism for unskilled workers during America's major industrialization – all these things have reduced people to being the marionettes of machine operating cycles. It separated employees from the responsibility for their work and its quality. The inner tie to a »work product« was replaced by an external monetary »compensation«, and the working people acted as they were treated: relieved of any responsibility for production and product.

This management paradigm has barely changed down to our days. The management consultant firm Roland Berger studied at German Telekom the way the order for a new telephone is routed. The form sheet went through the in and out trays of four departments. Up to 15 employees devoted time to the order – fragmented into many tiny tasks which specialists carry out with their specialized knowledge. Many are involved, but who is really responsible?

If responsible, then, at best, never open: at a magazine publisher I know there are seven departments involved if retailers send back unsold products for credit. Everyone moans about the work load. But in a narrower sense, the responsibility of responding to the order is not borne by any one single department.

The strides taken in internationalizing companies do the rest: at times the multiple assignments of overlapping regional, European, global and functional networks lead to a deeply felt lack of orientation among employees: »I haven't known who my boss is for months.«

Delusions of grandeur

In response to a guest asking the time the restaurant waiter replies: »I'm sorry, this is not one of my tables!« – The ability to relate to the whole: it is frequently completely absent in our companies. Many departments organize the work processes solely to satisfy their own needs without making the requirements of the whole process their guidelines. At the end of the day, what they expect from a department head is primarily technical expertise and experience! According to the studies done by Taubert, Henkel and Fechtner, managers pursue private and particular department interests during a large portion of their daily working hours. Frequently there seems to be no inclination to cooperate under one roof and for the benefit of the *whole* company.

That can be explained, for one, by the fact that the reward and punishment systems are massively individualized. But often this is also related to the shear size of the company, which in extreme cases is too big to grasp as a whole and seems beyond the scope of humanly fathomable dimensions. Especially in Germany there are the Jurassic Park of aged groups, the grandfather establishments with their traditional names glued together by the cement of gigantism. But how can responsibility and enormous organizations be compatible? I maintain: they cannot. People do not work in companies, they work in neighborhoods. These neighborhoods are defined by individuals in a »manageable« way. They encompass a certain number of colleagues, symbolic territories, local boundaries such as coffee break areas, hallways, lunch tables etc., as well as ritual procedures. Manageable units like these foster a sense of community and responsibility. On this level people define themselves for the company and, if any barriers are erected at all, they are against external competitors.

The larger the organizations and the less manageable the structures and processes, the less people relate to the whole. Anonymity, isolation, mounting hierarchies are among the complex costs of thinking big. To achieve something like a »we« feeling despite this, people put up barriers within the company: The earth walls and ditches are erected and dug *between* the departments – and it usually doesn't take long until management, with considerable effort, tries to weld together these exact same departments with »all-in-one-boat« slogans.

Large organizations are status-quo organizations. They set out for new horizons only on a rhetorical level. Even if you cut up this large structure and divide it into manageable company units, the new speed boats are quickly integrated into the fleet of a holding company which, behind closed doors, reinserts at least one additional hierarchy level and two rival competence interfaces. What a fun game of musical chairs!

Buried in the pyramids

If people are vain enough to accept the strains and stress of making a career for themselves they normally do not claim to want more power, status or money but that they want to »assume more responsibility«. Where can they get it? If you soberly observe our organizations then there is good reason to fear that they take it *away* from their employees. At the next management meeting the opinion will then be unanimous that the willingness amongst employees to show commitment has sharply fallen off. But is not always the response to this that managers should »relinquish more responsibility?«

Firstly, in order to prevent any misunderstandings: I believe in hierarchy. Wherever people come together they form, in my experience, relatively quickly and without much thought an (informal) hierarchical structure. When they work together in organizations, I therefore feel that it is both fair and practical (since it simplifies matters) explicitly to clarify the hierarchy. An explicitly stated hierarchy is at least bound by accountability. Whether it has to be so functionally interpreted, so thoroughly organized from top to bottom, specifying every minuscule incidental detail down to the style of door handles on cubicle doors, as is often the case these days, is another question.

On top the person who bears the authority, in the middle the manager who deliberates, and at the bottom those who add value: The current interpretation of the hierarchical paradigm is, however, old-fashioned, and sometimes outright ridiculously so. It assumes that employees are neither willing nor capable of organizing and monitoring their own work. That they neither can nor want to make decisions. The underlying message to managers: »Don't trust the self-monitoring of your employees, you bear the responsibility.« The commitment of the employee? Buried in the pyramid.

This is the reason why many archaic management structures from the days of early capitalism are still with us, which instruct, motivate and monitor formerly uneducated people in an environment which only changes at a slow pace. The hierarchically formal structures of work organization are like fossils from another geological era towering over a completely changed landscape of the present: four, five and more management levels between the working staff and top management perform competing tasks which frequently afford few options to choose from. The more management levels there are, the more monitoring energy there is – monitoring energy which contributes practically nothing to the addition of any value. On the contrary: it puts a damper on moments of success.

Companies are nearly the last feudal enclaves left in today's world. Just listen to some of these words: right to issue instructions – defined goals and objectives – supervisor – reprimands – chain of command – instruction – supervisory authority – subordinate. The German McKinsey boss Herbert Henzler: »The system still works according to the Clausewitz method: One guy says which way to go – and everybody else follows.« The mental image of Above and Below, the control metaphor dominates: »As a boss I think over what has to be done, make decisions, then I motivate the employees to carry it out. Finally I monitor the results and reward or punish accordingly.« The attitude: »I am the boss, so you do what I tell you to.« Ergo, the employees wait until the boss says something. »But I have accepted all the strains of a career for all these years only so that I can change something, so that things are done the way I want them done.« Of course – and that has its consequences. Employees attempt to appease the boss instead of responding to customers' needs. Or at least behave in such a way that they do not get into trouble. In various committees a lot of time is spent thinking about what the boss may want. In fear of spoiling their careers employees only say what the bosses want to hear and not what really matters.

This has a lot to do with the question: who gets promoted in companies? If you look over research studies you will see that managers spend between 60 and 80 percent of their time with work related to their professional backgrounds. To judge by their subjective attitude almost all of the people called managers are technical specialists who have been promoted. And they want to stay that way. Leadership? That's not work! That's something you do on the side! The result of this attitude is that decisions tend to be made one or two levels higher in the hierarchy than the facts demand. Individual responsibility is left behind. That is why the person most feared is the capable technical specialist: »What chances have I got if she is so good that she doesn't need any correction or close supervision?«

Similarly, no small number of managers think of their indispensability as the last bastion protecting their prestige. I am repeatedly surprised that managers cannot spend a single day in a seminar without having continuously to make phone calls, receive and send faxes, or quickly take care of this or that... Twice a day they call in while on vacation and get slightly depressed when they hear that everything is running A-OK even without them. But if managers are irreplaceable, they have failed. Then they are nothing more than good technical specialists – because the technical specialist is the only one who is »needed« on short notice.

I would like to present an example to illustrate how important the dismantling of hierarchies is in this sense: At the Schickedanz United Paper Works management began very early on with the organization of partially autonomous teams. The results were mixed. Quite a few employees had forgotten, after decades of little independence, how to accept responsibility. Only one employee group had no difficulties: the graveyard shift. The employees on the graveyard shift had been working for years already as a team without much of a hierarchy. The plant manager spent his time sleeping; they had to help themselves when something went wrong. One night worker related: »When I noticed one night that the glue for a tissue product was running out I left the plant at 3 a. m. driving my own car to get the glue from a plant in the neighborhood. 650 liters. My old jalopy nearly collapsed under the weight. But I got the glue. If that had happened during the day I would have had to fill out four forms, get three approvals and then place an order with a delivery service.«

His last will was his first

Can you still remember the Gladbeck hostage story? Shortly thereafter I had the opportunity to consult the police superintendents S and K in North Rhine Westphalia regarding the consequences in relation to the issue of employee leadership. The situation was clear: The police on the scene wanted cover and did not want to make a decision without an O.K. from upstairs. So they asked their immediate supervisors what they should do. They did not want to make a decision either and contacted their superior officers. The responsibility thus continued to rise upwards to the Minister of the Interior of North Rhine Westphalia, who had absolutely no idea what was happening on the ground. During this delay the gangsters staged a macabre media show to an audience of millions. On the one hand, the officers on the ground wanted to avoid responsibility. On the other, it became clear that higher ranking police officials had done quite a bit to prevent the officers from taking responsibility.

Take responsibility? This thought does not bring a sigh of relief, it causes people to freeze up: »No thanks – I was already responsible once, back in 1988!« This ambivalence towards accepting responsibility is understandable since it is usually accompanied by guilt and being called onto the carpet. Whoever officially accepts responsibility runs the danger under the existing conditions of having the guilt laid at their doorstep.

Many people are familiar with the enormous responsibility vacuum cleaner which always gets turned on when people think they have identified something going wrong. Hierarchy does not ask: »How can we solve this problem?« It asks: »Who's responsible?« Analyzing the causes does not lead to explaining the causes but rather to acquitting the collective by prosecuting the individual. Collective responsibility is difficult to make stick, so responsibility is usually applied to individuals because they can be held accountable. An example of this is the resignation of the person who accepts »political responsibility«.

This sets off the conflicts over where the buck stops: Who is to blame for this? The other guy! One of us has to change, and you're first! The present outsourcing trend is useful in this regard – it increases the number of possible »others«.

The joint and several debtors »at the top«

The reaction? People wriggle their way out of it, refer to special circumstances, conditions beyond their control and hope for special consideration. »Why me?« They defensively delegate the problem to senior management and duck back down into their cubicles. They expect »dynamic« leadership (whatever that is), »clear« decisions, permission: »Is this what they want up there?« At the top, the pressure to make a decision necessarily builds up, every detail and every possible individual is considered in the course of grappling with these »decisions«. The company's top management is then overloaded with responsibility which others have spared themselves.

Corresponding to the rejection of responsibility by the many is the complementary exaggerated feeling of responsibility by the few, who think they must have »everything under control«, although this overstretches their capacities. »Further down« people then complain about guidelines which are too strict. People who need not make decisions can usually speak unhampered by any consequences. The audience in the tribune can easily pass judgement. The calculated ethics of resignation of those who have clean hands because of their inaction is linked with the moral finger pointed at those who do something and frequently fail.

The joint debtors »at the top«: Whenever I confront managers – no matter what their level – in a seminar with alternative behavior patterns, they frequently, in their own inner monologues, are looking »hierarchically upwards«, thinking of their boss, relating to themselves as employees and wishing that others would also relate to them in the same way. They drop, so to speak, out of their leadership responsibility. Some have the courage to say: »I'm not really the right person. My boss should be sitting here.« If, at some later date, the boss in question is in one of my seminars, after a while, suddenly, he says: »I'm not really the right person. My boss should be ...« Passing the buck to »those at the top« reveals the long-term damage caused by an internalized authoritarian structure.

It is difficult to pluck out the song of commitment on strings stretch across a hierarchical framework: a hierarchy demotes any sense of responsibility. »The board has resolved, ... I do not agree with this, but what should I do?« – People who say this, are stealing. Out of their responsibility. He shifts the responsibility to a higher authority and neglects to mention that he said »yes«. His employee has to bear the consequences. But if the employee must execute this policy then the boss, in fact, agrees with it. At one large food concern people can evade responsibility with a single, stereotype sentence: »This is what America wants.«

Cover your ass

Accusations of guilt, expiation, suppressions: The hierarchy-specific persecution mentality programs employees bureaucratically to pass the buck. Superficially, this may appear in the form of detailed procedures to assure decision-making quality. But the over-inflated back-up institutions, the commissions, the many signatures on letters, the columns of recipients on memorandums, for the purpose of getting many people involved: these are all memoranda to evade responsibility not to make decisions. It is all a back-up effort whose meaning is: »But you were told!« The irresponsible use of the passive tense rules internal corporate correspondence: »Due to the current situation it was resolved ...« Recipients: all. Author: address unknown.

When difficulties arise people are glad to bring in consultants. To avoid the responsibility for the drastic cut backs in jobs. »How can the problem be formulated so that I can stick to my solution?« It is not infrequent that managers buy justification studies which give an external blessing to decisions already made. The door-to-door sales reps of acceptable corporate futures rapidly achieve the productivity increase goals, initially. Possible counter-productive consequences do not arise until later. Others will have to deal with them. The employee reaction: »We survived McKinsey twice; we will also survive Boston Consulting.«

Cover your ass. This means primarily applying the tactic: »Eliminate the symptom as quickly as possible, not the problem, for nothing is as effectively distracting as a quick fix in the wrong place.« And for re-thinking the basic approach, the time is always ill chosen. First you have to create the prerequisite for the prerequisite for the prerequisite. Ideally, someone pushes through rapid decisions and insures that they are considered changes. What counts here is the ritual of »getting something passed«: guidelines and rules are ideal for this purpose.

Evasion tactics I: guidelines

Accordingly, a confidential entry in the biographical film script of many companies is: »Regulate as much as possible!«, as if people had an incurable drive to seize the nearest rope, like climbers in a blizzard. The fact is that many companies would have collapsed long ago if employees did not frequently enough loyally reinterpret, re-shape or even simply ignore detailed instructions: »The top brass has no idea what's going on down here.«

All the guidelines are written in response to specific conditions, mostly to prevent everyone from doing something which only *a very few* do or would do – and they do it indirectly anyway. Such guidelines rarely help people or encourage them to do something. Even more rarely do they support the acceptance of responsibility.

As a result, a guideline not only hampers creativity, it also inhibits employee responsibility. Flexible working hours, for example, frequently celebrated as the triumph of fantasy over rigid organizational structures, is based on the idea that employees can protect themselves from exploitive demands of their blood-sucking supervisors by referring to their working time account. There you have it! Long live responsibility!

Attempts at internal corporate standardization: If the ISO standard has been met, that does not mean by a long shot that the company is producing quality. In this instance control processes are described as ideal types, standards are met, the bottom-line orientation roars in victory over the skill orientation. The quality assurance mentality cuts off the feedback line from the marketplace and defines quality »internally«. Characteristically, the word »customer« does not appear in any single standard. What is certified is quality management. The whole nicely hierarchically structured by the management with the help of the quality assurance task officer to the quality management overseer. Every time people get absorbed in their handbooks they are directing their energy inwards: Do the employees know which rules are being set down for them and where? Because these are the three underlying principles of the ISO 9000 ff.: documentation, documentation, documentation.

There are companies in which the target agreement culture is over-worked to such a degree that the whole job is regulated with up to 30 target agreements annually. The need for security on the one hand, and the need to control, on the other hand, erects the walls for the work place as an internal death-row prison cell.

The slowness of many decision-making processes is related to the fact that every control problem is immediately regulated. While BMW must wait eight months for a building permit in Germany, a comparable permit in Japan, in an area where earthquakes are common, takes 6 weeks. This reveals the notorious guideline overgrowth. This is also a drag on decision-makers. The drag-net of ordinances, rules and operating regulations is a trap for any responsibility. The individual may initially feel rage and impotence, but that is followed by increasing calm, and a slow limp towards early, personally declared, retirement. Any remaining enthusiasm is stuck in the tightly woven steel nets of regulatory mechanisms best summed up by the words »That won't work.«.

Internal entrepreneurship becomes increasingly an internal battle against regulations and policies. In search of excellence? In search of mediocrity! In brief, I can no longer bear to hear the whinging about the shortage of entrepreneurial personalities if each and every control problem is immediately knocked dead with a guideline. What remains is a cemetery of enthusiasms. Should we not be disturbed by how many young people who took on a task in the company, bright and motivated, frequently after a mere two years have withdrawn into an inner retreat? Many of them have, so to speak, a mask on, playing the game only on the outside, while inside they are far from recognizing it as »their game«. Those present, because they cannot find anything better, have already left.

Evasion tactics II: committees

If you identify key processes in the company, analyze them and search for the people responsible for these processes, you'll be looking for a long time. Where their initiator is eroded, diffused like some Magellanic cloud of blurred responsibilities or completely eliminated, there can be no authorship in any meaningful sense. Where can accountability, where can responsibility be identified? The deep layers of hierarchy and the broad spread of responsibility lead to the fact that nobody has responsibility anymore.

In the case of Schneider, the property speculator, it was nearly impossible to identify any person concretely responsible for the risks involved in extending credit. At Deutsche Bank there was – not least colored by decades of learned carelessness – a high degree of structural diffusion of responsibility. In addition, the prioritized harmony commandment in the board of governors equally distributed the responsibility in case of damages to all the decision makers.

Within companies many feel hampered by, and at the mercy of, institutions and committees which are nearly completely depersonalized. Usually this starts quite innocently: If you want to promote a certain issue in the company, the first thing you do is set up a team. Usually there is, somewhere in the company, an executive officer who really does not have a task of his or her own. He is then assigned the task of heading total quality management, high performance organization, lean management, human resources development, corporate communications, business reengineering ... or whatever else happens to be the latest leaf on the growing branch on the tree of empty phrases. This manager then develops an extraordinary, high-power approach, igniting firework campaigns which quickly fizzle out, but call attention to the importance of the issue (and the manager's activity), controls line managers from the sidelines, and is felt to be a nuisance, a know-it-all and a disruptive influence. The company's management feels relieved: »Now we have someone right for quality management.« They know they are with it. The team managers have specific responsibilities firmly to establish their raison d'être – and complain at the same time that the line managers refuse to accept any responsibility for this specific issue. Since the management fashions are continually changing, one can imagine where this leads. There is truly no shortage of impulses and external ideas. But there is a shortage of responsible implementation. Before the action of one wave has time to take effect, another is on its way, which will also dissipate across the sand.

The next step is the project group. A committee or a body of experts is established. But many of these »We have to do something about that« projects merely appear to be active; whoever happens to have time becomes a project participant. Often there is not even an overall head who represents the group to the rest of the company and defends it; the line managers affected by it disturb its work whenever they want; the project goal is unclear; what is the problem on the agenda anyway? The Board must have had something in mind. If the results do not meet the Board's expectations, there could be unpleasant consequences, then *there are* consequences: The project group is dissolved. The top management usually remains excluded from genuine processes of change anyway. Top management waits for things to change »down below«.

And »down below« they wait for permission signals to come from »the top«. And so both are waiting. A lot has to change, if they want everything to remain as it was. Now is the time to start!

Over 30 years ago, David Ogilvy put it like this: »Take a walk through the parks of your city, and look at the statues there. You will only find Nelsons or Bismarcks, and never a committee for achieving this or that goal.« No doubt the future belongs to the integrated, i. e. function-overlapping business team. But that must not mean that the responsibility is diffused. Nestlé chairman Helmut Maucher is right when he says: »Teams with a Leader« instead of »Teams as Leaders« – which should not be confused with monological decisions to shell from the commanders on the hill.

Responsibility

»Responsibility: a removable burden which can be easily passed on to God, fate, accident or your neighbor.« Ambrose Bierce puts the popular defense strategy in a nutshell in a refreshingly derisive manner.

Colloquial language itself differentiates active responsibility »which someone takes«, from the passive state of »being held« accountable for something. The first basic meaning defines certain areas of responsibility for tasks and functions, especially including the consequences and by-products of activity. This *task responsibility* is actively taken and gives people opportunities for self-actualization and proving themselves. That is the bright side of responsibility.

The second basic meaning, accountability, is proceeded by a question which suggests an accusation. It is accompanied by the suspicion that one of these responsibilities was neglected. In addition – in most cases – the person is threatened with liability. This is the dark side. If the task responsibility tends to have a neutral to positive significance, when people are held accountable they are up against a wall. Individuals face a tribune and fight for their reputation, their integrity, their career opportunities. Here they can expect an acquittal at best, but never an evaluation.

This is the explanation *why* the organized evasion of responsibility spreads like an epidemic: because in many companies the secondary accountability side dominates the primary responsibility for tasks. Furthermore, because the whole phenomenon is viewed essentially in terms of risks related to accusations and liability, both types of risk are avoided even more since many companies have cultures where persecution is the norm. In those companies responsibility is frequently a matter discussed only after the horse has bolted. A culture of making others look like dolts is the rule: »Looks like you don't have your department under control!«

But in the company *each individual* is basically responsible. On various hierarchical levels, in different task areas, in different functions. The acceptance of a task is, in practice, a promise. Whoever accepts a task irrevocably commits themselves to carrying it out and to be held accountable for any defects. This self-commitment applies at all times. If you want to avoid responsibility, you must therefore avoid the tasks, that is, the individually assigned tasks. (The best way to do this is by joining a *TEAM: **T**errific! **E**veryone **A**ctive but **M**e!*)

For Otfried Höffe, therefore, responsibility means in summary the »responsibility which (1) rests *with* someone, (2) *for* something, (3) *to* someone and (4) according to *the specifications of* certain evaluation criteria«. Then there is the personalized responsibility in a legal sense, the functional responsibility, political responsibility, the responsibility towards parties outside the company, within the company ... None of this is individual responsibility.

Individual responsibility

The issue of »individual responsibility« had already been on the agenda before the lean management concept visibly pressed the hierarchical pyramid into the shape of an onion in nearly all companies. Vague as the term is, it can be used for everything and anything and seems to contain a predilection for something morally upright. Individual responsibility is talked about primarily when it is absent. This, in turn, is thanks to the described Janus-faced character of the second of the two words.

Applying Höffe's definition, criterion (3) applies here; people who are individually responsible are initially and primarily responsible to *themselves*.

This means: towards the company you are faced with a choice. You can assume the role of an observer; the company is then, for you, the »environment«. But you can also take on the role of a participant and view the company as »your environment«. As a participant you »take part« in the responsibility. This decision – and only this – is the situation of responsibility. It is the situation of the absolute necessity of responding. Do you want to remain an observer and view the company as an environment? Then the relationship remains one of I-THEY opposition. Or do you want to enter a relationship with your company as your environment? Do you want to be a participant? If you choose the participant role then a partnership, an I-and-YOU relationship arises, which is characterized by equality, participation and responsibility.

The daily, practical meaning of responsibility thus simply designates the readiness to recognize responsibility when it has not been previously standardized in a clearly defined task assignment. Of course, you can regulate employees so that they remain seated at their workplaces five days a week, 8 hours per day. But what you can never regulate is whether they will show responsibility in their work. They must choose to do this and want to do this. The fewer managers there are and the larger the span between the levels of hierarchy the more important it is for employees to act on their own responsibility.

The will to take responsibility. The freedom of choice and the self-reliance of repeatedly re-negotiating the substance of one's level of participation. The motivated involvement in one's work, experienced as positive and self-actualizing, not as being »victimized« or as fulfilling a »duty«. The satisfaction gained from individually transforming reality, which opens, and maintains new areas of dialogue: individual responsibility means the readiness to actively take on room for manoevre, aware of the potential dangers and opportunities. Am I prepared under certain circumstances to make substantial sacrifices? Do I put myself on the line and demonstrate civic courage? Do I avoid being continuously pushed around by others? *What is the meaning of commitment in the company if it does not mean responsibility for one's own motivation?*

Thus, individual responsibility basically means:

- autonomous and voluntary actions; *choice*
- action arising from initiative and involvement, *will*
- creative and innovative action, *response*

Commitment

There are terms whose meaning withers as they come into general use. Much of what is meant by the term commitment remains largely unknown in German companies. The German term for individual responsibility, »Selbstverpflichtung«, is dressed in a penitent's robe and brings to mind asceticism, sacrifice and renunciation (the root of the word »pflicht«, meaning duty, is probably the cause of this). The meaning of the German term for individual responsibility is largely the same as commitment. Certainly, at a conscious level it is also understood to imply a promise and duty, and can perhaps best be illustrated in German cultural tradition by Friederich Schiller's poem entitled »The Promissory Note« [»Die Bürgschaft«].

This sense of commitment includes the terms autonomy, involvement, creativity as well as the promise »I'll do it!« So commitment encompasses acting on individual responsibility and being aware of individual obligation.

The whole scope from response to civic courage: The attitude of the individual who experiences responsibility not as a burden but as a source of satisfaction – that is commitment. Martin Heidegger appealed to his students at the end of the 1920s: »We must recognize: at this point in time we do not have any grasp of an objective, generally binding truth, or power; the only support left available to us is attitude.«

In the following presentation my concern is to contrast the desert of organizational irresponsibility in companies with the oasis of commitment. Individual responsibility is the life-supporting spring which enables us to live in the desert without having to relinquish to it. People who neglect to fill these oases with life, those who flee from their own responsibility into passive discontent, contribute to their own oases also becoming deserts.

Then the sentence »That's the way it is« need only be supplemented by »So what can I do about it?«

The Philosophical Section

An old, old story

And Adam hid with his wife under the trees of the garden. God called Adam and said: »Where are you?« He answered: »I heard you coming in the garden: I grew afraid and hid.« Then God asked: »Did you eat from the tree whose fruit I forbid you to eat?« Adam answered: »The woman who you gave to me to be my companion gave me of the tree's fruit and so I ate it.« God spoke to the woman: »Why did you do this?« The woman answered: »The serpent seduced me, and so I ate of it.«

Fortunately the serpent cannot speak. Otherwise it probably would have said something about the attractive loveliness of red-cheeked apples which were impossible for it to resist. (»And anyway why is an apple just hanging there in the first place?«) Does God allow Adam to bite into the apple to show that he has bitten more off than he can chew?

If it is true that the world's great religions reflect basic human characteristics back to us then the shifting of responsibility to others started very early on in human history. Anyway, since then we have to work. Driven from paradise, we earn our bread by the sweat of our brows and battle against thorns and thistles. But at least it is not boring anymore.

It is revealing that God neither guarded the tree of knowledge by high walls nor an angel with an ever-turning fiery sword. Everything else is left to the free decision of the new human actors. To complete a work of creation which would please Him, *our* Creator? The story liberates the creative new interconnection of choice, will and response: the cast form of human creative ability, the basis of human work.

In this light the expulsion from paradise appears to be the craft of reason: it enthrones mankind as the completely responsible creators of their »own« world. Are we prepared to exchange the counterfeit currency of our illusions for the sound coins of responsibility? In relation to God and to life the situation is clear: there are no excuses.

Choice

> *The responsibility for everything which you do, or neglect to do, starts and ends with you.*

»I work of my own free choice!« – The ironical quip from an elderly manager surprised all those present. Me too. Surprised because he merely pointed out the obvious but connecting »work« with »free choice« is linguistically unusual, an apparent contradiction in terms. It tore open a level of meaning which is buried under the daily busy-ness: »autonomy« or the »freedom of choice«.

I would not like to discuss this subject on the open field of academic thoroughness but in *practical* terms. How can reflections on freedom of choice be useful for commitment in the work place?

Individual choice

If people talk about »choice« in connection with business then most people think of the fact that some time or another they selected this company, preferring it to other companies. Perhaps purely practical, down-to-earth considerations played a role in their decision, the commuting distance, the closeness of family, friendships. Later the word choice is only used together with the word »no«. There is a ring of helplessness about it.

No choice? Careful! The path of inner self-justification leads us directly into a blind alley. Let's take a snapshot of the situation:

> *You have freely chosen*
> *your professional situation, the way it is now.*
> *And that means you yourself are responsible*
> *for the consequences of your choice.*

This may have a cynical ring in your ears if you are in conflict with unappreciative colleagues or your always unsatisfied boss has once again treated you unfairly. But, looked at carefully, you have allowed your current predicament to blind you to your basic situation.

The basic situation is: by acknowledging this thought you decide about the freedom – or lack of freedom – in your life. Perhaps you wonder what the above thought has to do with the freedom in your life. Well, if you recognize that you have freely chosen your professional (and, of course, your private) situation you can also leave this situation again – at any time! Sometimes just the mere thought can make people feel lighter. By thinking like this they consciously assume responsibility for their lives. With all the consequences.

Whoever now feels a »Yes, but ...« on the tip of their tongues, I would ask to exercise a little patience. My intention is not to individualize with royal indifference all the suffering in this world by pointing a finger and claiming »That was your choice!« and maintain that the surrounding conditions are unimportant. Of course this broad generality can be presented in much greater complexity as soon as I sympathetically introduce relativising considerations such as: things are not as simple as they seem. Many decisions are complex, the consequences are not foreseeable, there are the so-called compelling circumstances, and there are many other valid objections. Fransisco Varela discusses the fact that our acts are frequently just »immediate coping behavior«. There are paradoxes: Ortega y Gasset's »Freedom is being forced to decide«, breaks, ironies: »Sorry my car is driving so close to your front bumper.« I would like to respond to all these »Yes, buts«. But I would like to begin modestly by stating that the attitude described above is simply *practical* for your commitment in your work life.

Again: this company, this boss, these colleagues, these employees – all that and all the other conditions and surrounding circumstances in the company: you chose them. No matter what motives you had, no matter what your reasons: you picked it out. You chose everything as it is, by making your decision to work there.

No matter how you look at it: you always choose where you live, the type of work you do, what significance you attach to your career. And: you are free to discard it. If you want. Perhaps you do not want to for good reasons, and these reasons are so substantial that you are prepared to put up with the considerable irritations it involves. Decisive is: you can always change your decision. If you, for example, do not reject the company for which you are now working then you do not *want* to reject it. It is exclusively your decision and responsibility.

I am still shocked today by the apparent banality of these sentences. But if we observe the concrete behavior of people in companies these thoughts seem to be difficult to digest. Thus I have spent a large part of my working time with people in companies who – firstly – may *want to do everything* but – secondly – *do not want to pay the price for it*. By necessity, every choice has consequences which we simultaneously also choose. There is no trick in the world which allows us to avoid these consequences. But that is exactly what everyone seems to expect. Moreover, if that does not succeed, *cannot* succeed, they all start whining. But people who whine do not want to be responsible.

This is precisely where the greatest opportunity lies: people who stop whining, act. People who act, choose consciously. People who choose consciously assume responsibility for all the consequences. People who accept responsibility, take their lives into their own hands – that is nothing other than freedom. And you secure it for yourself.

A fresh start every morning

Allen Wheelis, whose essay »How People Change« helped me considerably to arrive at this idea, wrote: »Nothing guarantees our freedom. Deny it often enough and, one, day, it will be gone. Finally our feet and hands are tied and we exclaim triumphantly how right we had been.« The problem is indeed that most people in companies have forgotten that they choose. They even choose on a daily basis. The simply forget that they decide in favor of this company every day. That they can also decided against it, if they want, but do not do so for reasons *for which only they are responsible*. That they choose this boss, who perhaps does not really correspond to their own expectations, every day, repeatedly. That they say »yes« every day to this one employee who they fly into a rage about at regular intervals.

The department next door which is so incredibly lame that it gets hopelessly lost in thickets of detail – they choose it every day; the salary, which is naturally always a little too low, that is also something everyone chooses at the end or beginning of the month.

It is helpful to review in our minds all the choices which we make every day. Every employee in the company makes a large number of decisions on a daily basis which are relevant to productivity, which, depending on attitude and motivation, can impact one way or another. »Should I finish this calculation today or is there time until tomorrow? Should I stop by the potential customer or take it easy? Should I wait until I have been contacted by the neighboring department or should I initiate action myself? Should I go to work despite my slight cold or should I »put my feet up« for a few days? Should I inform my colleague about difficulties with customer XY or should he find out for himself?« These decisions are usually made *unconsciously*. Exactly because they are frequently made unconsciously we hardly notice them and they lie forgotten in a dark corner of our daily awareness. If this unconscious choice is uncovered, then people say »Of course!« – and then it is immediately forgotten again.

Conflict, for example: if one person does not want to fight, two cannot. Nobody can force you into a conflict. You *choose* the conflict. You can also reject it with the words: »Let the garbage float by.« If you do not want to do that then you want to get something which the conflict can provide. People do not get involved in a conflict if there is no advantage in it for them. But this is precisely what many do not want to see: »He forces me to take steps against him!« Nonsense: nobody can force you; you decide for yourself.

Power, for example: many people perceive themselves as being powerless. Especially in conflict situations, e.g. with their own boss, the feeling of helplessness and powerlessness dominates. A misunderstanding. Let us plow the jungle of powerlessness! For matters of power always involve two as well: the one exercising power and the other who permits the former to exercise power:

Power can only be granted.

You grant your boss power over you. You do not have to do that. In extreme cases you can even reject him. (Elsewhere I go into the question of whether you might be better off accepting your boss as a challenge.) But if you do not want to reject him – and certainly for good, respectable reasons! – that is also the result of your decision. Nobody has power over you. Reject powerlessness! The real person in power is always yourself.

I realize that appearances contradict me. But, according to the rules of our economic system, you have also chosen the possibility of being moved, promoted and fired by your boss. For leadership can perform magic. But you can too: anyone who has rejected a boss or a company knows the feeling of liberation which suddenly and seemingly immediately arises. Everything which was once so incredibly important, pressing and determining in life, vanishes. As if someone had turned out the light. None of it retains any meaning, it is as if it had never existed at all. Sometimes this feeling is worth remembering. And sometimes it is worth repeating the experience. Louise Beal wrote: »Love your neighbor, but choose your neighborhood.«

Whenever you start to complain about the boss or the company – then you have forgotten that you chose it. (Which does not mean at all that you should not make any and all attempts to change an annoying situation. But more about this later.)

Keeping quiet

The problem with the Pied Piper is never the piper, it is always the rats. As long as there is no resistance any boss can assume that the employee agrees with his decision. Otherwise the employee would negotiate and, if necessary, choose not to cooperate. I know companies in which everyone moans – but they are all still there. Why?

Suffering is easier than acting.

But suffering is only easier than acting for those people who have suppressed the awareness of freedom of choice. Despite this, they are still responsible.

Each individual is not only responsible for what he does, he is also responsible for *what he fails to do*. How often, after a conference, have I heard this whining sound which starts even on the way to the parking lot, cutting to pieces the resolutions just passed. In the conference itself, however, the same people, so intent on criticizing now, did not open their mouths. But afterwards they feel they have the right to criticize the resolutions. Organized irresponsibility: these resolutions were made with and by them. They also chose the consequences of their silence. It was their decision. People who, wrinkling their noses, stand aside, believing they always have a better solution in their pockets, but do not present it, and make everything else look foolish: They are the gravediggers of a living company.

I am not speaking here of whether it is clever that a boss in a meeting puts all his rhetorical eloquence into supporting something in the face of conforming employees. I am speaking of the individual responsibility for decisions which come about as they do because of our silence. We must loyally support decisions after they are made, if we continue to choose this company, the playing field for which these decisions apply. Especially we Germans should have learned: the dictator never creates the conditions. The conditions always create the dictator.

A very eloquent image for this thought was painted by Hans Blumenberg as a complement to Aesop's fable »Scolding the Ocean«:

The shipwrecked man, thrown up on the beach, awakes from the sleep of exhaustion and finds the ocean is calm again. He becomes enraged, and scolds the cause of his demise. The sea replies to the angry man: »Don't scold me, scold the winds, for my nature is no different than that of the land. But the winds drove across me and stirred me up to make the wild waves«. Aesop's fable ends there. Hands Blumenberg continues it. The winds, criticized, should have had a chance to answer. For example: »The sea is not like the land. If we drive across the land it does not budge an inch. If the sea were not obedient to us, there would be no waves, no shipwrecks.«

Who is worst off?

How do I motivate myself? – That means, firstly, making conscious choices and assuming responsibility for the consequences. Difficult enough – when people have perceived themselves as victims of circumstance, perhaps for decades. For most people in the company are not aware of their freedom to choose. Ultimately they believe they *must* do what they are doing. There are doubtless many considerations which undermine the individual's freedom of choice: the frequently unconscious, even preconscious source of the act of choosing in the past (»I did not choose that, that happened to me!«); the consequences and results of our life's path up till now (»I'll never get out of this rut!«); the limits which tradition and habit burden us with every day (»We always do that this way here!«); the plans for the future to which we have linked our expectations and hopes (»I want to become director of business operations next year«). Also arguments which sound like this: first spring fever, then the summer slowdown, followed by autumn depression and winter hibernation.

Frequently fear is involved. Since the alternative undermines our security, since we often do not know what is awaiting us, we attempt to justify the status quo with all the means at our disposal. An auto-suggestive hide-and-seek game takes place: »That is not possible because ...« This is how we run on the spot, trapped in the »No choice!« treadmill. Rainer Werner Fassbinder's lived logic in the film »Fear Consumes Souls«: to avoid fear, we deny our own power to choose and allow ourselves to become the plaything of an apparently inescapable self-emasculation.

The apparent »advantage« of this self-emasculation: the others, the circumstances are to blame! »Freedom means responsibility; that is the reason why most people are afraid of it,« said George Bernard Shaw at one time. The self-proclaimed victim frequently finds an impressive number of »rational« reasons, which – met with understanding nodding of heads all around – simply left him *no* choice than to submit to the dictates of others or the prevailing conditions. Those who whine have a further advantage: they are among colleagues. They are never alone. Whinging is a contagious, epidemic virus which many people voluntarily let themselves catch. Unanimously faint-hearted: the function of whinging as a social bond should not be underestimated.

The danger to career plans, or of even losing one's job, is the ace of trumps in the popular company game: »Who is worst off?« Besides, it is generally thought of as »normal« to be dependent on someone – if for no other reason than out of consideration for the family. In an excited tone of voice one hears: »You have it good; I'm not doing this just for myself, I have to think of my children.« It is not easy to convince someone, who, self-emasculating, is comfortable in the leading role of his helpless victim story, to accept the idea that he has chosen all of this for good reasons which are not at issue here. Because *he* considers it right and important to act in this way. It is nobody's business to pass judgement on his reasons. But he is responsible for the consequences.

Anyone who wants to make a new choice today, can do this. They must only be prepared to pay the price. But aren't they already paying the price today? So instead of feeling like the victim of circumstances, as impotent, it is much more practical to compare the prices, and then to decide for the one or the other. However you decide, and for whatever reason, by doing so you have consciously assumed responsibility for your life. A responsibility which you have anyway. How much better it is to be aware of the fact! That separates the self-emasculated from the self-empowered. You decide yourself, which group you want to belong to.

Choosing consequences

We do not always choose consciously. A lot of unconscious choice is mingled in. Unconscious, primarily, since we consider the consequences of our choice *in terms of possibility*. We are hardly capable of anticipating in every situation all the effects of our decisions. Are there perhaps more difficulties awaiting us than prior to our decision? Sometimes just the costs of obtaining the information seem too steep. But a decision without any risk is not a decision. And it is impractical to complain about the fact that something unexpected, not calculated, arose and thwarted our plans. It is much more practical for a stable commitment not to become dependent on the unexpected.

Let us consider a rigorous example as an illustration: I remember very clearly the lament of some top executives in the North Rhine Westphalia steel industry whose positions had been seriously threatened since 1992. Well, it always was an illusion to believe that the market is an all purpose solution for job security. Whoever was working in the steel industry at the beginning of the 80s must have been aware of the fact that his job was under threat due to the crisis in the industry which had been looming for years. To start complaining when job cuts actually took place is at best humanly understandable – but it is not intelligent. It was forecasted. But independent of this fact: whoever works as an employee in a company, is *basically* always at risk of losing their job. This is part of the game which they chose. In complete contrast to the self-employed. The latter has chosen another game. But also they must consider other risks: not receiving any contracts and, thus, becoming unemployed. But even this danger does not really exist; there is merely the danger of not being able to do *this type* of work any longer.

Certainly people who think security is the sole navigational buoy on the river of life will have a hard time accepting the thought of the capacity to choose. The feeling of being imprisoned dominates such people. Many have furnished their lives so luxuriously that it seems altogether absurd to risk any of it. Chains of gold are as binding as chains of iron. Indeed, the price from the point of view of the individual can be extraordinarily high. That is not my concern here. By no means do I want to suggest that people sacrifice their comfortable standard of living and the security of solid, material well-being. The problem is that many are not prepared to accept responsibility for the effects of their staying put, to recognize this as the result of their own decision and to accept immobility as the price for this decision.

You always have the basic freedom of choice. If you feel responsible for your company, then you have chosen this responsibility. You can also let it go. Whether that is ethical or unethical, right or wrong, is not the subject of this book. But if you have chosen, then you are responsible for this choice, that is: you must bear the consequences. Furthermore, it destroys one's own feeling of self-worth to complain about these consequences. It is similar to raising children: it is not difficult, but it is frequently difficult to live with the results.

Objections

»I guess I have no choice«, said Billy the Kid resigned, looking into the barrel of the Sheriff's revolver. Let us transfer this scene to our playing field for those readers for whom principles are all important: »I have now twice turned down assignments which the board of directors offered me. Recently I was offered another assignment

– this time abroad. If I also refuse this one I can forget about my career.« One of those famous »Offers you cannot refuse«.

Actually he can. But he does not want to. Our executive thinks the presumed price is too high. That is why he decided to accept. No doubt this is understandable. Whether it is smart I don't feel I can decide here, but I really doubt whether it is ever smart to say »yes« under such pressure. But even in extreme cases we must allow for the fact that the person who assumes a certain role in the company does this on the basis of his own decision. Under certain circumstances he must pay a high price if he refuses. But in fact he only compares the prices.

Or the banker who is entrusted by his company with setting up a branch office in the new German states and complains about the many difficulties and his family problems: »But I cannot just let this assignment drop now, when I have just started.« Yet he can. But he does not want to. *Other things are more important to him.* Nobody has the right to assess for another that this or that price should be weighed as lighter or heavier. That is exclusively a question of personal values. Where one would quit his job, the other just responds with a tired smile. If you can live with all the conditions in your company, except with the fact that, for example, the parent company in the USA dictates the guidelines, then there are hundreds of jobs where this is not the case. You can go there. If you can live with all the conditions at your company except with the fact that in response to the smallest drop in sales the budgets are drastically cut, then there are hundreds of opportunities where that does not happen, even hundreds of jobs where you need not answer for any budget at all. The basic truth is:

A person who says »I cannot«, does not want to.

Managers – like the one above – frequently justify their move to another country to their family with the fact that they had »no other choice«. I do not want to trivialize the decision-making process which is often like an emotional roller-coaster ride. But the fact is: once you have decided one way and whatever you feel, you have chosen against the interests and claims of your family in favor of the presumed interests of your company. Perhaps this clarity threatens your self-assigned role as a good father. Perhaps you want to be considered a caring father despite your rejection of the needs of the family. Then you ought to consider using the well-known trick of telling yourself and others that, in the end, you really did not have any choice. Wrong! You did. But you don't want to stand up for your decision. Like children, who believe they cannot be seen if they close their eyes.

A visibly irritated manager: »That's easy for you to say. I built a house here in town. My kids are still going to school here. My wife has a small shop nearby. And besides: at the age of fifty where am I supposed to find another company? They are all looking for people under 40.« I consider this a serious objection and some readers will label my arguments up to this point as »theoretical« and classify them with a smile as a sort of academic game of marbles.

But the argument does not touch the core of the issue. This manager does not want to pay the price either. But far be it from me to recommend that he give that all up. While many in the course of years have doped themselves up with so many material opiates that merely holding on to this comfort requires immense sacrifices and seems to have completely buried any freedom of choice. But thought out to the end: this person does not want to sacrifice all that, but is, on the other hand, prepared to work at a profession which has not satisfied him for a long time, and to work with a boss who makes his life unbearable. He is willing to pay *this* price, but not the other one. This is a decision. He can also make another one.

Let us consider an extreme case, and everyone can judge their own situations: what prevents you from accepting the dream job as a sailing teacher in the Caribbean? You yourself, all alone. Nobody else. You do not want to do without the conveniences of your fully air-conditioned security container. And there is certainly nothing to say against that. But do not blame your family, the circumstances ... all of that you *can* leave behind, if you want to. If you do not want to and continue living as up till now, then do it with the awareness that you have chosen to do so. Then there is no longer any basis for blaming something or someone else and for »I cannot do that because ...« Seneca says: »Not being willing to is the reason, not being able to is the excuse.« Hard, but true? No: hard, therefore true.

»Everyone does what he wants to do.« A statement which is associated with general chaos and which even the fashionable chaos theory cannot raise to the level of order, is really a fact. You always do what you want to do, and never what others want you to do. In this light Luther's famous excuse must be modified to read: »Here I am, I can act otherwise!«

Other people's expectations

The demand of the boss to increase sales in the coming year may trigger general excitement. Quite apart from this you decide for yourself whether you want to meet this demand. You can do it or not. Either way you are responsible.

Other people's expectations are what *others* expect. The drama does not start until you start making other people's expectations your own as a reflex. The need to please and obedience in anticipation of an order are frequently the disastrous consequences. But if you are obsessed by the fear that some top shot may no longer like you and will block your career opportunities, you make yourself into other people's plaything, and give them power over yourself. You alienate control over your life. You are not on earth to fulfill other people's expectations.

A second drama begins if you belittle other people's expectations. You need not do this at all. For everyone in the company has the right to expect acceptable performance or behavior. In my experience only a minority of employees would be so impudent as to try, for example, to call into question the columns of figures of the cost accountants. In sales and marketing the situation is different: most employees believe they have intimate knowledge about these matters and can add there two bits. No reason to get excited! Of course they can get involved and formulate their expectations. But *you* decide how you will act.

And in response to the demand for a 20 percent sales increase under difficult market conditions? The answer of a field employee who has chosen responsibility is: »Of course I will provide a 20 percent sales increase next year. To do this I need the support of a budget amounting to X, the sales promotion action Y and support from marketing Z. You do not want to make these prerequisites available to me? Then I will not make any commitment for the 20 percent. I only make agreements that I can meet. And please: do not mistrust my willingness to perform!«

Jargon of irresponsibility

I have the impression that the more or less conscious refusal to choose – especially if the necessary choice can really no longer be put off – is generally on the increase in business. Decisions are left unmade. But procrastination is silly. The attempt to have everything at once, not wanting to sacrifice an alternative, is costly: delay is time's thief. Oversleeping favorable opportunities. Frustration. Being internally torn between alternatives. And this too was a decision: indecisiveness. »People must also decide to hesitate«, says Stanislaw Jerzy Lec. The real problem is again the refusal to accept the responsibility for the consequences of indecisiveness. Typically such employees say things like: »I had to...«, »I was obliged to...«, »Actually I am not permitted to...«.

But people who say »I should...« never in fact do. They replace acting by a sharpened awareness of problems, by a »clear view« of things. Widespread among marketing research and marketing discussions: *wanting-more-information-than-is-necessary-to-act*. A cheap way of ducking responsibility. The energy flows into making explanations, into interesting knowledge. The reasoning pretends to be action. In this way people believe they can remain passive: understanding things instead of moving them. The results: a decisive »Maybe!« The unspoken self-depreciation: »I am always making the wrong decisions.« – »I'll never be excellent.« – »I cannot decide.« These people make themselves unhappy. For *one* consequence of indecisiveness is always the loss of self-respect. No »poor decision«, no matter how negative its results, can balance this price.

Even worse are those people in business who declare themselves to be the victims of circumstances with phrases like »I could not ...«, »I had to ...« or »I had no alternative.« »I don't want this, my boss does!« That is the jargon of being sucked into a situation. These people make *everyone else* unhappy. They have lost the consciousness of freedom of choice.

»... we are compelled,« is something people say who want to cover up their responsibility either unconsciously or to manipulate others. And the cowardly »I'm afraid I must inform you ...«: it is extraordinarily difficult to work with this type of employee, because in their view objective conditions in the company are always at »fault« and must be changed. They do not think of examining themselves. They do not see that they are the source of their own problems. They are, in part, not even prepared to recognized that they are seriously damaging themselves with such an attitude: on the battlefield of the subjunctive.

The concept of »trying«

Directly revealing in this connection is the talk of »I tried ...« or »I'll try ...« (Try to close the book that you are holding in your hands at this moment! No, don't close it; you should *try* to close it.)

Trying is an attitude which wants to avoid responsibility. Logically there is no such thing as trying. You either do something, or you do not. I am not so concerned here with the linguistic convention but with the inner attitude which does not want to accept responsibility. It is similar to »good intentions«: nothing but self-deception of the clear »I don't want that!« I really want something else. But I do not have the courage to admit it to myself and others. What I really want, I do. I do not have to plan to do it.

The »try« strategy is correspondingly often used to cover up passivity and weak decisiveness. In my experience people talk very frequently of »trying« when someone really wants to say »no« to a demand but fears the consequences of clarity. So they try it. Many say, for example to some target or other, »yes«, think »no« and anticipating failure, build in bugs (while working) in advance. They ought not to be surprised then, when they are extremely successful with the concept of »trying«. They always try. But they never do.

When Reinhold Messner, after the failed attempt to climb a mountain in the Himalayas (he decided due to oxygen problems to turn back 100 m below the summit) was congratulated for his attempt he answered: »I didn't try. I was not on top.« No victim story about hazardous conditions. No heart-breaking story about the enormous, but finally unsuccessful exertion. No plea for sympathy for a case of bad luck. A clear: »I was not at the top.«

Difficult choices

I am very aware of the fact that in one deep cellar of this thought structure cynicism is lurking. Sometimes the difficulty of making choices is a choice in favor of difficulty. For all fundamental thoughts of this kind there is the danger that the braided rug of argumentation may start unraveling at the edges. And there are not few readers who vigorously reject what has been presented up till now as the blasphemy of an anti-social devil. Some may think they recognize the satanic features of cut-throat capitalism.

Even if someone may believe, he can only chose between the pest and cholera (although he in fact has more options): the fact is that there is only one thing we cannot choose: choice.

In my seminars, participants often feel the idea of freedom of choice as an unreasonable demand against which they defend themselves with whatever comes to hand. As soon as I have developed the idea people start looking for holes or contradictions in the model. People get lost in the deepest extremes of existential situations to disprove the universal validity of the principle (although I am solely concerned with the usefulness of the idea). Life and death are not things that people choose (many so-called »primitive peoples« and world religions see this differently); and it is certainly not possible to speak of choice in relation to illness (although western medicine has already clearly established the role of individual responsibility for psychosomatic disorders). But what is important is not this or that »scientific opinion«. The question is whether a thought weakens or strengthens your individual responsibility.

Circumstances? Difficult choices

But there are circumstances beyond our control! Really? Is not pointing out this fact more a matter of lazy thinking, a spurious argument, an avoidance of responsibility? Frequently enough, »time pressure« has to play the role of culprit. That people produce it themselves, that it results from individual choices, that there is frequently nothing more behind it than the lack of courage to say »no« – this fact is passed over in silence.

However, under the pressure of the economy and deadlines, freedom of choice is rarely experienced. Steven Brenner and Earl Molander were able to show as early as 1977 that 43 percent of the managers surveyed felt compelled to engage in practices which they morally disapproved of but found necessary in order not to endanger the success of their company and, thus, of their own career. The title of a report in one influential manager magazine read like a suggested guideline: »Managers who pollute the atmosphere against their will«. Nonsense! Nothing happens without you wanting it. You have made your choice.

Especially when executives want to reject the wishes and demands of their employees, they frequently base their arguments on »circumstances beyond our control«. The refer to »external circumstances« in order not to answer for their »no«. Or they wash their hands clean in innocence and pass the buck up the ladder: »I really do not want to do this at all, but I have a boss too, and he is forcing me to ...« The only person doing the compelling here is himself. But his hands must remain clean. That a choice lies behind this is not mentioned – but generally speaking this fact is also not clearly confronted.

The talk about compelling circumstances opens the gate to hordes of cynics. These are people who sense that they compel themselves, that the compelling circumstance is only an excuse but do not admit or allow any feeling of suffering. »It is difficult to know something and to act as if one did not know it« (Wittgenstein).

The Grand Inquisitor in Dostojewsky's »The Brothers Karamasov« – you can visualize him as the classic illustration of this type.

Cynicism is closely related to burn-out, a syndrome which has received a great deal of attention. Even seminars are offered to support the prevention of that creeping process of internal burning out whose symptoms are lower capacity and productivity, depression and an increased susceptibility to illness. At such seminars they talk about the lack of recognition, stress, poorly organized work processes, socio-emotional impoverishment and the absence of meaning. One pamphlet includes the observation: »if someone must tolerate an intolerable situation, without being able to escape«. Victim stories! The real source of the phenomenon is that people are not aware of their freedom of choice, and have not come to grips with limits on their autonomy (which they have, however, chosen). The feeling of being helpless and not – as it should be called – of having accepted helplessness.

But people who have accepted helplessness can change their situation, at any time. They have the alternative of exposing compelling circumstances for what they always have been: compelling people. People compel themselves and each other. To become aware of this is especially important in an age when people label mendacity as »honesty under the pressure of circumstances«.

For the sake of completeness: people working in business know that economy for a large number of people has rigidified into »compulsion«. For many the word freedom is a mere advertising gimmick; they refer to the machine-like character of the world, the codes, the large organizations in which individuals twitch to the rhythm of interactions. The pressure to conform is often experienced as overwhelming. But what *is* has not always been that way. Neither will it remain like that. This fact should also encourage us to think about *changes* and progress in business – and not only to think about it. I will return to this later.

Destructive ideals

All ideals have a highly destructive dimension. They blind us to what is possible because we fantasize about unachievable goals. Feelings of well-off citizens who look at their closets bursting with clothes and sigh: *my wardrobe is always incomplete!* Similarly, no matter how good our company, our boss or our employees are, they always fall short of the ideal we have set for them. In secret we take vengeance on them for not being the way we think they ought to be. The attention revolves around the unfulfilled expectation. It is as if the others were only on earth to make us happy. Many work overtime with what amounts to a self-destructive rage on their overdemanding expectations to be able to justify their complaints and objections about prevailing circumstances and conditions. They are constantly on the look-out for the hair in the soup. Moreover many sit shaking their head so long at their soup bowl until a hair falls in.

These people bring their »searching«, latently unsatisfied attitude to each new job. It is surprising to observe how people switch from one company to another, permanently looking for the »right« opening, always hunting for the ideal job, not recognizing that they themselves are the problem. They forget that they, so to speak, »supply« the deficit themselves. For them, something always seems to be missing. The glass is always half empty. But we ought to put paradise back where Christians have always thought it was located: in the hereafter.

This is not an argument against changing jobs or companies. However, some people reach a deceptive conclusion: they think that by changing jobs they will find a position greater or better than what they already have. They dream of life and work situations full of satisfaction, recognition and material well-being. They pack their bags, say goodbye to the old company (not infrequently envied by their former colleagues) and, in the end, wake up in another company – and there beside them are the same selves, unchanged, who they ran away from. Their selves stay with them no matter how far they roam.

If you believe that by an external change of working circumstances you can find something which you do not have within yourself, you are travelling away from yourself and getting lost in external appearances. But soon you will again be accusing the circumstances which again are not to your liking. But *No boss is there to make you happy*. If you are dissatisfied with your job and private life then you have forgotten to accept responsibility for your choice.

People who think like that have also forgotten that there is always something missing from the ideal. They could turn their current work into the only right one for them. But that blocks their basic searching attitude. Soon they again have the feeling that they are missing something crucial. That real life happens somewhere else. That they are waiting at the wrong train station. People searching outside themselves would think of even the most terrific profession in the world as, at best, second rate. Searching is an attitude. Not finding. After a while they will continue on their journey: traveling is the fool's paradise, says Ralph Waldo Emerson.

Consciously choosing

What makes choice so difficult is having to do without the discarded alternative. That is the familiar situation of the decision neurosis. Should I take the job in Hamburg or the job in Munich? Should I decide for this or that applicant? Should I pursue this or that marketing strategy? Should I continue diversifying the product range or concentrate? Torn between two lovers: a choice must be made between two different options. Choosing means: one door is shut! The word »forgo« in itself causes distress in an atmosphere of fun-addicted pastimes. It even has an odor of a stale virtue, of days gone by.

The expectation is very wide-spread that it is possible to get everything at once without having to pay the price. »I want everything!« – »It would be fine, if only ...« Considerable energy is then invested in fantasies about the discarded option. Or people take a defensive attitude towards the loss of the discarded alternative by discrediting the side rejected (the familiar sour grapes): »That would not have worked out anyway!« – »Who knows what would have been awaiting me there!« This sort of activity is not genuine choosing. For example, many professionally active women weaken their own position by discrediting women who are »only« housewives. It is not until we appreciate the alternative and then decide, keeping both in mind as serious possibilities, decide for one path, that our decision has both power and dignity. Bert Hellinger wrote on the subject: »If people scorn what was not realized, it takes something away from what they chose. It is made smaller. If they honor what was not realized, even though they did not choose it, then they add something extra to what they have chosen.« It is practical to think in these terms: not until we appreciate both alternatives does a choice have power. Otherwise it is not a choice, but an escape. Saying yes to the price adds something valuable to what we have chosen.

You always choose whether you are aware of it or not. But conscious choosing is precisely what lends the choice its dignity. Genuine responsibility thus emerges from a *conscious* choice. As the wise man said: *decide what you do and you will do what you decide.* Nevertheless, without the certainty that all working situations are the results of my choice, »free will« cannot be understood. John P. Carse writes: »But people who believe they *must* play, cannot *play*.« It is impossible to chose anything if you *must*. If you must, then you cannot decide in its favor. If you believe you have no choice, then you cannot take on responsibility.

If you experience yourself as the victim of circumstances, you shift the responsibility to others, and you yourself are not responsible. Then commitment will never become part of your vocabulary. Commitment means: being aware of your freedom to choose; being aware that you have chosen everything as it is. Worded negatively: *without awareness of freedom of choice no commitment is possible.*

Milhaly Csikszentmihalyi's research findings demonstrate in an impressive manner that work satisfaction can only be deduced to a very limited extent from external conditions. Its real source is elsewhere. You yourself are the source of your satisfaction, not your work. To experience pleasure in your work you must be prepared to stand 100 % by the situation as it is *now*, to acknowledge it completely, to say »yes«. Not because it would be the »right thing« to do. Not because some outside authority had declared this to be morally valuable. But solely because you have chosen it, and because you are aware of your choice. That – and only that – is the decisive step towards commitment.

From my first boss I learned the laconic question which he always asked me with a gentle penetrating voice whenever I again complained about the world's shortcomings: »What is the alternative?« If it is »Do nothing«, I knew at least what I did not want.

So if at the end of this chapter you have more unanswered questions than when you started that would not necessarily be a bad thing.

Will

Practice makes perfect.

»In Robert's case I often experienced how he will rise from the lunch table, his lips moving slightly, walk to his computer, enter something, sometimes returning in silence as well, but occasionally simply not coming back.«

»You might say, Mike works 12 hours a day and more; you could also argue that he does not work at all.«

»Dr. Brettschneider – he would still hurry off to his wind tunnel if he had won the jackpot in the lottery.«

»I still remember him well – no spectacular actions, but persistent and tough. Without making much of it. Many of us did not properly realise how important he was until he was gone.«

»Definitely: Tina Behnke – she once rented a small airplane to deliver goods to a customer on time.«

»With one VW employee I once experienced how, without warning, he crossed over to the other side of the street and set right the windshield wiper of a VW.«

I had invited seminar participants to describe to me people who they would call »committed«. These are some excerpts. I could have added many more. They show something which is closely related to energy, concentration, decisiveness. In contrast to the classical physical definition I describe this energy here borrowing from Artistotles: »Energy is what sets everything in motion.« Energy is a process – not a substance or thing. We cannot observe it directly, but we do experience its presence. It is present in everything that we do, and for that reason often escapes our attention: »The most obvious fact about energy is that there is nothing else.« (Lawrence Blair)

Energy can be experienced. In one seminar, a manager remembered his first boss: »Whenever I spoke to him I had the feeling: this discussion is important to him now. I am now, for the next half hour, his most important partner. He was highly concentrated, present and alert. And this was not a show or fake. I always felt rewarded after such discussions, even if sometimes the talks were somewhat rough.«

We can experience this commitment energy in how people do something. They do not seem to have any motivation apart from doing it. Children at play are a good example of this: parents know how difficult it is to call kids to the table at mealtime when they are absorbed in a game.

Usually this is expected from people whose professions can be performed under favorable, external conditions: flexible challenges, large latitudes, creative design work. The research into satisfaction, no matter which approach it comes from, disproves this in no uncertain terms: even in the case of work which would be described by most people as boring, dull and unimportant there are repeatedly people who see opportunities, unseen by others, to develop abilities, which others would never have thought them capable of, and thoroughly enjoy their activity: apparently it is not the external situation, but how it is subjectively experienced, the attitude, which determines the experience. How is this dedication to assignments, how is commitment, possible?

Action strategies

I would like to invite you to draw up a list of the specific shortcomings of your everyday work: what is it that you do not like about your job? You will quickly have identified a few conditions which ought to be nicer, better, more pleasant, fairer. Perhaps some of these shortcomings are in relation to your »ideal self«, including: skills you would like to have, talents, characteristics ...

What can be done if you do not intend simply to uncork a bottle of homebrewed »Hope«? I would like to offer three options of how these shortcomings can be corrected. The first is the most important: *change something*.

Do not be satisfied with the status quo. Take the initiative. Be a »misfit« in the positive sense of the term and stand up for your own interests. We have enough conformist yes-people in business: the ones who have refined and perfected the »Please the boss!« approach and obey anticipated orders to the point of complete self-denial. You can display the highest degree of loyalty towards your company by supporting changes of things which disturb you.

Our routines, our business knowledge and »functioning« have, for most people in the company, reinforced the attitude, that working life, as they experience it, is something necessary and »natural«. In addition, standard orientation patterns, as expressed in the term »outbid« or the rhetorical figure »top-bottom«, are accepted as if they were anthropological constants and left unquestioned. Employees often do not understand themselves as »actors« in a creative sense, as people who shape the social reality of business.

All the present »things-as-they-are« are not as obvious as they may seem. If we do not want simply to accept the present and experience ourselves as passive and powerless, it is helpful to question this apparent obviousness. The structure which has frozen up must be changed back into what it really is: problem solving in time. The entire present is defined as having grown historically, as a result of people's decisions and creations under very specific historical conditions. To this extent it is subject to change by people time and again. That which is, is only one of many possibilities. To paraphrase a familiar Adorno quotation: »Only someone who can *also* think of the present as different than the existing present, can dispose of the future.«

Of course I know that in many companies a more-or-less open battle is being conducted against misfits, eccentrics and non-conformers. Employees who are highly motivated and act because they want to are frequently seen somewhat disapprovingly as »obstinate«. But in this chapter I am not encouraging knee-jerk rebellion which seems to »need« the others in order to work out a sort of forced anti-conformism. Nor do I mean blind rage or the popular fundamental opposition: being basically against-it all. I mean the vigorous »drilling into hardwood boards« which Max Weber once described. The persistent improvement of a thousand small and large problems, burdens and difficulties. Do not wait for others to do it for you. These are *your* drawbacks which you sense against the backdrop of *your* values and interests as faults. Thus you are also the one who can make the changes. Sometimes it is helpful to compare your »inner« job description with your job description on paper. If they do not correspond to each other it is time to modify the one on paper.

Perhaps you are now thinking, somewhat condescendingly: »Your roar is impressive! But I have already frequently tried to change something in my company: nothing happens.« Everything said, impossible, a hopeless case. Then one option is still available: *leave your company*.

If something is really important to you and there is no possibility of achieving it in this company then there is no reason to put up with it. On the contrary: there are so many companies which offer interesting fields of endeavor and which could possibly make something available which suits you. There are so many fields with challenging bosses, friendly bosses, without bosses, with generous freedom of action, best pay, without any deadline pressures, in beautiful residential areas, with skilled employees, etc. Nobody wins if, grinding your teeth, you obstinately stay put in a position of rigidified tolerance: not the company, because having a half-hearted employee is like having a rotten apple in the basket. Not your family, because your latent discontent will certainly be felt there too. But primarily not you: you are wasting your life.

In a company which has been 100 percent family-owned for decades I had the opportunity to chair several board meetings – until it became clear to me that the expectations of several members of the Board absurdly assumed that the company should *not* belong to the family. The board members were not prepared to recognize the facts as they were: *what is, is.* At some point or other changes cannot be made. There are situations in life, which cannot be changed now and by individuals, which must be recognized if people do not want to end up like Michael Kohlhaas. Then the normative power of facts rules. Then we are faced with the decision whether we can live with the existing situation or whether we wouldn't be better off to leave.

In this situation you may spontaneously react with the sentence: »I cannot leave!« The underlying message here is a little different: you do not *want* to leave. Something else is more important to you. You do not *want* to pay the price of a change. There is nothing to add to this. Nobody has a right to assess the reasons for your remaining. But then your complaint is not really very important to you. In any case, not so important that it causes you to act, that you overcome the fear of the risk involved.

What would happen if you got completely out of the business? What would be the worst thing that could happen? Do you expect to be unemployed, are you afraid of a loss in status, a bruise to your career? Would you loose your self-respect because you believed that you had failed? I am not trying to take a moral position in this context. My interest is in defining the price involved. It is the fear of the unknown which prevents us from risking changes. Nothing hypnotizes people as well as their own fear. The path leading away from fear, however, is directly through it. It is even probable that at the point where we feel the greatest fear our greatest treasure is buried; the feeling of cheerful composure and freedom; the feeling of doing something not because we *must* but because we really *want* to.

But if you say to yourself: »Yes, there are a few things which are not acceptable for me in this company, but that is no reason to leave it,« then you can still choose: your *inner attitude*. You may not be able to direct the wind but you can trim the sails. People unable to change an unfortunate situation should at least be intelligent enough to change their attitudes. Of course you can continue to bemoan yourself as a victim. But another option is more practical: *Love what you do!*

Do your work with love and devotion! Not because the job is so great, the conditions are optimal or because someone else higher up said how valuable the assignment is. But simply because you decided to do it. For no other reason. Whinging and not dealing with the matter at hand, always focusing on the negative – by doing this you are dragging yourself down: people who complain become a burden to themselves. Do what you do with excitement and enthusiasm. Enthusiasm comes from the Greek »en theos« = one with God, roughly: »with God's energy«. Say »Yes!« loudly and clearly to your work.

Or forget it completely.

In London in the early 70s you could read the three levels, succinctly worded on t-shirts:

Love it, leave it or change it.

In some companies this sentence is common coin. However it is frequently shortened cynically to »Love it or leave it.« They then give up one of the most important employee potentials: the ability to be creative and innovative. They suppress the desire to change, to improve and design.

The Becker Factor

Some readers will shrink at hearing so much emotive language that he feels is contained in the immediately preceding paragraphs. Some others will think they hear the music of the spheres intoned by esoteric self-discovery folklore. Love – that sounds like ambrosia therapy, research into extraterrestrial circles in cornfields and reincarnation gymnastics. Indeed, the word love in the German language is a linguistic embarrassment, even frowned upon in the soberly staged objectivity of business life. Accept, yes, but not love! By love what is meant here is: *doing something with your whole heart*. To decide against the half-heartedness which has become a principle in our companies. To be completely involved in the matter at hand. »For nothing is worth anything for people as people if they cannot do it passionately,« Max Weber lectured his students.

What is meant here can perhaps be made clearer by a statement made by Boris Becker – in his best years without doubt a personification of commitment. Unlike any comparable player one could see by the way he played whether he was really whole-heartedly in the game. When at one early high-point in his career (1989) he won the US Open in Flushing Meadow under adverse conditions he said in an interview afterwards: »You have to love this tournament if you want to win it. You have to love it despite the air traffic noise over you, you have to love it despite the hysterical audiences, despite the concrete landscape and despite the tortuous heat. Like Jimmy Connors loved it 18 years long. If you cannot love it you had better leave the court.« Becker also sees what is wrong; he can certainly imagine more ideal working conditions; but he knows he can only win if he fully recognizes the conditions as part of the game, if he does not tie up his energy in whingeing. Energy which he might need to win. That is the Becker factor: the ability to concentrate completely on the here and now and not to waste any energy. To do something whole-heartedly. Even while clearly seeing the things which are not O.K.

Or Jürgen Klinsmann, who during the friendly match against Uruguay (Oct. 1993), after several punches from his opponent behind the back of the linesman, was flat on the ground. After the game an extremely excited reporter asked: »What do you say about that?« Klinsmann, relaxed and sober: »That happens to me again and again in this position. It would make no sense to get upset about it. I don't think it is any good either, but today it is simply part of the game.« To avoid any misunderstandings: This is not a license for unfairness. We must do everything we can to prevent this. But if, for whatever the reason, a situation is like this, then we can decide for or against it, whether it pleases us or not. It is simply not intelligent to complain about how it »really« would be better otherwise.

This is not the basis of a covenant with existing conditions, beautifying intolerable conditions. It is not a question of remaining passive, painting a gray reality in rosy colors or to practice the deception of smiling, shrugging our shoulders and saying, mechanically, »Think positive!« (Though this is unfair to the term positive: »positive« which comes from the Latin word »positum«

and means see and weigh the whole, including the negative.) But the point comes when you – at least for a time – must recognize the power of what exists. This not only applies to B. B., and not only to the »grand slams« of your working life.

Some of you will say: »I cannot afford to lose this job.« But:

Work either picks you up or drags you down.

If you do not love your job you cannot afford to keep it.

The Power of Love

The »amateur«, from the Latin »amare«, or to love, is someone who loves what he does. Due to being spoiled more and more with extraneous rewards and substitute drugs a condescending shadow has fallen across this term. Are the amateurs hopelessly naive, or, when they review their personal happiness balance sheet, can they consider themselves the real professionals? An employee working in the conveyor belt business at Kali und Salz AG summarized the point as follows: »I would also do my work if I did not have to feed my family. I simply like it.«

Love is, what love does. Love is the doing, is activity. Love is not a feeling that overwhelms us but a decision which commits us. (I do not mean in this context the confusion arising from falling in love.) Feeling love for something or for someone is frequently considered to be something spontaneous, which just »happens«, sometimes even against our will. However possible that may be in a relationship – love demands everything which is a prerequisite for any satisfying human activity: discipline, patience and endurance. If love were a feeling, then the many loveless deeds of people who claim to love would be inexplicable.

Thus, love cannot be separated from will. If you really love, then you do so because you *want* to love. It always involves consciously directed, purposeful energy.

Many people in this context make reference to duty. That is respectable. But they mean something different. There is no love in duty. In the term duty there is the aspect of imprisonment, limitations on freedom, paying homage to moral standards which, over the long-term, destroy the individual's substance. There is always a seed of hatred towards what or whoever seems to be preventing us from self-determination in our lives. While nobody has so much power over us, we frequently would like to shift the blame onto someone else and look for ways of secretly obtaining a reimbursement. A little every day. In the company we then become one of the business extras. As long as we see ourselves as forced to do something, because it is our obligation, we do not love it.

Rigorously thought out, there is no such thing as obligation. This claim is somewhat brash, I know. But every obligation you receive from someone else presents you with a choice. If you »accept the obligation«, this is your choice. It is always a self-commitment, even if you experience it in the context of forced and mandatory. You then have usually decided not to like this commitment. But you ignore the fact that you did not like *your decision*, and that you can decide otherwise.

Unfortunately, executives often believe that they are obliged to tell their employees what they should or should not do. What they call duty, sometimes even responsibility, is part of the training and superiority convention which they worship. What results are the highly conformist lackeys with too little responsibility, slavishly obedient, whose mediocrity top managers complain and laugh about. To »fire them up« a whole battery of incentive instruments are thought up whose consequences I have described further on.

Taking another small step forwards, another illusion is hidden under the term duty: »I am only doing it for you!« Seen in the context of commitment: *You have never done anything for someone else*. Your actions may have been useful to others. They may have promoted and strengthened others. But, basically, you act because *you* consider it right and important to act this way. Because you have chosen it. Because you have decided in favor of acting this way (and not for another way of behaving). Because it corresponds to your values and standards.

Taking action always satisfies a need. It is always *egocentric.* I do not want to put anyone down who helps other people. But this helping does not get its power from outside, not from a why, but from a whence. People can commit themselves to the well-being of others for the most deceptive motives – as Herbert Witzenmann repeatedly pointed out. If you say you are doing something for your kids, for example, then that is deceptive and meaningless. You are acting in this manner because you are demonstrating responsibility for your decision. Furthermore that is precisely what should be respected! Not the »for your sake« number which, anyway, amounts to indirectly assigning guilt or exploitation. One manager related, after he had thought about this idea: »My son once made me feel terribly ashamed when I excused my increasing working hours with the words: ›I am doing all this for you‹, and he replied: ›No, Papa, you are doing that for yourself.‹«

The only organization which we all work for is »I«. This does not legitimate any lack of consideration. This does not excuse unsocial behavior. Moreover it would be erroneous to believe that such an attitude is cold and without feeling. Just the opposite is true. All our wickedness is based on our addiction to controlling others: e.g. by extortionate good deeds which compel them to thank us and make them dependent on us. The »I« describes the point which researchers in ethics have long recognized: »Ethics only have a chance if they are based on egoism. Only this sort of intelligence-based morality does not demand too much of people.« However unkind this may sound to you, only this sort of clarity makes commitment possible. So do what you do, and do not expect any thanks.

As a result, it is self-deception (often also an extortionate intention) if you think you are doing something for others, for the boss, for the company. Then you are denying your own responsibility. Everything you do, you do for yourself. »Selfless commitment?« – I have never understood what that could possibly mean.

Strength of ego and individualism have always been treated as degenerate and unsocial. That they could go along with freedom, creativity and commitment, that enlightened individualism is not identical with lack of consideration, that a market economy is opposed to a power-based economy – all these thoughts are more at home in the American philosophical tradition. At a time when the trap of a new period of restoration is again opening everywhere in Germany, when the spirit of the times is to denounce »exaggerated« individualism as a reflection of crumbling values and the erosion of social stability, where a re-formed social control is meant to impose the meaningful »community« over the supposedly meaningless »society«, it cannot be said too clearly: the »old« company with its fixed structural and integration patterns cannot be saved.

It must be re-designed to meet changed conditions. What is more, this reconstruction must be born by trust in the ego culture. This is the only way that individual responsibility and commitment are conceivable in communities. That ought not be confused with »social frigidity«. It is a matter of changing the philosophical framework in companies to the extent that individual responsibility is encouraged. That has very little to do with rhetoric. But a lot to do with leadership.

The secret of motivation

Modern companies are nowhere as blind as when they consider the question of what motivates people. You can unleash as much technological power as you want: when it comes to the sources of subjective energy a complete lack of interest dominates. What is the source of passionate and persistent energy? It certainly is not external incentives such as premiums, bonuses, praise and criticism or other drugs. If we make use of these kinds of stimulants we may feel a short burst of sufficient energy but no sooner does the effect wear off than we drop back into our earlier condition and become increasingly dependent on our internal company drugs. Over the long haul it destroys the living energy in us. The fire which is ignited and fanned in this way, is also blown out.

»Commitment is,« according to the Coca-Cola manager Robert W. Woodruff, »when you do not care who gets the laurels.« – »Pretty retarded,« some people may now think, and yet the intended meaning is on the mark: People who act, in order to be rewarded (or at least not punished), are at the same time not »mentally alert«, but dependent on other people's praise and criticism, thereby letting other people have power over them. They deliver in response to the carrot and stick approach. People who perform work for an audience in a tribune must consider the possibility of a thumbs down. Whoever makes his commitment dependent on the applause from those around him is a wet dishrag. He may grow old, but he will never grow up.

If someone can motivate you, then he can also discourage you. Then you are inviting everyone possible to determine your standard of living. Others then have power over you, and you have lost your self-respect. It is therefore crucially important to assume responsibility yourself for the energy and the satisfaction you bring to your work, and not let yourself be »motivated«. Only if you, yourself, assume responsibility for your motivation can you avoid being discouraged by conditions, customers, colleagues, briefly: the others.

Any motivation other than performing whole-heartedly what you have chosen, lands with mechanical certainty in frustration, discouragement and internal company drug dealing. To a greater or lesser extent, everyone has such motives which lie outside the actual work. But to amplify them cannot be either in your interest nor in the interest of your company. Even in the mid-term, the readiness to perform sinks. The motivation factor of »fear« (of the loss of the premium, recognition, the career chance, the job) throws a cold shadow. At best, only Roman galleys can be commanded like this.

Energy, dynamic force and intensity are, as a result, only imaginable as a »self-willed« action, never as an action resulting from secondary considerations, controlled from above or outside or in response to rewards. Energy is where freedom of choice is experienced.

One or two readers will perhaps still vaguely remember the law of conservation of energy from their physics class. It states that the total sum of all energy remains constant, thus energy cannot be created from nothing and cannot dissipate into nothing. Energy can only be modified. Since the quantum theory was developed many researchers therefore prefer the term »interaction« over the term energy. Precisely this interaction is what happens at the workplace, in fact in any facet of life. If you do something with love and devotion, you experience happiness and satisfaction *to the same extent*. Of course you can also take care of tasks with half as much energy; the result will correspond to that: half-hearted results, an absence of joy, mediocrity. That is the secret of motivation:

> *You get back from life what you put into it at any moment in time.*

The Beatles wrote the lyrics on their legendary White Album: »All the love you take is equal to the love you make.« It is easy to trivialize the naive flower power romanticism; what it says, is: We are responsible for all happiness – including the happiness in our work – which »comes our way« (how irresponsible our language is) in this world. We are our own soundboxes. We only get back what we give.

Working in order to live?

When do we feel this energy? When, as we fall asleep, we are glad that we may arise the following morning and continue. Furthermore, when we do not reserve this feeling for our hobbies, but for all the hours that we are alive. For to divide something into one part, which is, and another part, which should be, is a deceptive way of leading one's life.

But that is precisely what many people do. »Do you work for a living, or do you live for your work?« In disputes in the diners between the customers at the counter and the table reserved for the regulars to establish who knows better, this question is usually quickly dealt with: »That's obvious: I work in order to live.« If you look at it a little more closely, it is usually clear that the time at work is felt to be time controlled by someone else, not infrequently as »sold life«. (This atmosphere is still alive in personnel departments: when formulating remuneration policy they talk about »compensation«, now referred to in Germany with the English word; economics still uses the term »work burden«.) The energy investments are then moved from the company to the private sphere. The complicated »in order to« rules the mentality: work, in order – afterwards – to live.

Is that practical? It is extremely impractical! Just imagine how much of your life you spend at your place of work. People who have lost interest here, are really lost. If you do your job with only 60 % energy, you defraud yourself of life. If you sit at your desk and dream about Hawaii you are neither at your desk nor on Hawaii. You grow ill or destructive, or both. You do the best *for yourself*, when you do your best. Then you are no longer accepting a job but providing work.

Discipline – concentration – initiative

Energy also contains characteristics which come close to a hostile provocation in the post-modern paradigm: discipline and concentration. A person on the summit of a mountain did not fall there. Without self-discipline no problem can be solved. It is necessary for every kind of learning and growing. Menuhin said once: »If I do not practice for one day, I notice the difference. If I do not practice for two days, my friends notice. If I do not practice for three days, my audience talks about it.« An ancient Zen koan says: a master is one who practices.

Joy – that is something different than short-lived amusement! – can only be experienced as the result of high attention and, in Elisabeth Noelle-Neumann's opinion (rarely do I agree with her), never the result of unconcentrated, wandering animation, never the arbitrariness of pleasure, it always goes along with making effort, overcoming difficulties, eliminating obstacles: »Happiness can only be achieved by growth in energies.«

The learning company must, if it is to function properly, be a disciplined (and not a disciplining) organization. All decisions, problems, conflicts are growth opportunities. But they are linked to pain, to forgoing. The English word »decision« comes from the Latin »caedere«, which means »cut off«. Decisions always also include sacrifice and doing without. The tendency to avoid problems and the suffering they contain is the main reason for the neuroses in our companies. What makes this so difficult is the illusion it should be easy, painless: the ideal workplace, the ideal boss, the ideal company, the ideal employees are waiting for us. It is sometimes difficult to keep agreements. It is sometimes difficult to follow the game rules in the company, especially in an age when breaking rules is considered a sign of autonomy. Challenges and difficulties, giving up habits and anachronisms, shelving old ways of thinking and acting, being open to change: all of this is felt by many as unpleasant – and avoided.

If we take a look into the display case of military tradition we can find Clausewitz who is also repeatedly cited by hard-liners with relish: In the heat of battle, when life and death hang in the balance, the point is to concentrate one's own forces on the right point. In the »fog of a more or less sizable uncertainty,« which each field commander must tackle, what is required more is decisiveness rather than a brilliant mind; alertness triumphs over the unexpected. Concentration therefore, of which people oddly (I know no explanation) often say that it is »oblivious«: that is the ability to bundle all available energy like sun rays through a lens.

An anecdote on this subject: An American friend who visited me in Germany and, at that time, still spoke somewhat broken German, said one morning: »I will attend to the radio today.« Diplomatically I corrected him: »we say: listen to the radio.« »I know«, he insisted, »but I would like to attend *to* the radio.« I did not understand what he meant immediately; it wasn't clear to me until later: concentration – that is the difference which characterizes commitment.

A somewhat removed example of this difference might be a comment made by Bertrand Russell regarding the philosopher Ludwig Wittgenstein, that as a soldier in WW I he »would have never noticed anything so unimportant as exploding grenades when he was thinking about logic.« Thomas Mann, who every day – really *every* day – wrote from 9 until 12; even – as Wolf Schneider reports – as the furniture packers around his desk were emptying his study; Franz Schubert, who in 18 years up to his early death composed 23 piano sonatas, 19 overtures, 18 string quartets, 15 operas, nine symphonies, seven masses and more than 600 songs in 7 working hours per day; Thomas Edison, whose innumerable failed experiments did not prevent him from finding the right filament; Sigmund Freud who sovereignly continued to write even after 23 jaw operations; Ernest Hemmingway, who rewrote some of his short stories dozens of times and did not touch any liquor until he had written exactly 1000 words.

»But I am not a Hemmingway«, you might think. (»But primarily not Mr. Müller from controlling!«) Of course – these recorded examples are of the geniuses of world history. But I would like to avoid conveying the impression that commitment is something sublime, spectacular. Do we all not know people, quite normal people, who *do what they do* decisively, patiently and persistently? People who act with passion? Who even under the most unfavorable external conditions can lead lives full of warmth, love and confidence? Who are totally and completely involved? Are committed? *There is no absolute yardstick for commitment. »I« am the yardstick.* That also means the readiness of a person to make personal sacrifice. The important fact to remember: the individual does not *experience* this as sacrifice. Of course there are limits. But nobody can say where these limits are at the outset.

From the survey mentioned above:

»Some days she is only in the company for a few hours; but in her mind she is always working on her plans.«

»He simply does not let up. If he wants to clear up an issue, then he wants to clear it up, no matter what the cost. Sometimes it is very irritating.«

»He is not presumptuous, but when you deal with him you always have the feeling that his current project is the most important in the whole company.«

If you read them carefully, the opinions address, without exception, *activity*, not position or job. There is apparently a difference, whether we like the conditions, the character, the symbols of our work, or the substance. »I like being a salesperson« is not the same as »I enjoy selling.« »I love being a director« is something different than »I love facilitating people to achieve success.« Before you disqualify this as semantic nitpicking I would like you to check how many people in your own immediate surroundings love what they really do, or the conditions, the status symbols, the monetary compensation. If you want to distance yourself from people then you should, at most, distance yourself from people who love their job. Never from people who love their work.

In business, terms such as »discipline« and »love«, examples such as Thomas Mann and Franz Schubert may seem wide of the mark; but: the same basic principles apply. A closely related term is »initiative«. Initiative which grows out of the insight that total security is an illusion. In addition that no matter what you lose, you also always win something – if you are prepared to recognize the fact. This is the reason why the widespread yearning for security contains a large measure of self-destructiveness. That is why the company pays for the efforts to attain security – however sensible at first glance everything from the ISO-9001 to the 7 total quality zero-error programs may sound – the price: initiative, courage and a readiness to take risks are threatened and may get lost. Granted: agreeing to quality standards is helpful. But we need initiative much more urgently! An initiative for the initiative in business: entrepreneurial initiative, technological initiative, mental initiative.

What we need is an awareness environment centered around individual initiative. Do employees develop their own ideas? Do they pick up on ideas? Do they follow up on what they have started? How independently do they work? Do they wait for delegated incidental assignments, or do they look on their own for missions and goals? Do they think about changes within their own spheres of activity? To what extent do they obtain the information they need on their own? Do they also remain concentrated in situations of unusually high pressure? With employees who, like gatemen at railroad crossings, are always waiting for the whistle, we will not be able to keep up with future competition. Therefore: do you promote initiative and civic courage? Or do you provide examples which show that the conformist is rewarded?

The ambivalence of goals

Well, these initiatives in business are primarily thought out with an eye on some corporate goal or other and the result is that people are looking hard into the future. Reaching a goal at (almost) any price is often the unspoken solution of many corporate cultures. The path to the goal is frequently underestimated, while the contributing company processes, the »How« of achieving the aim, often remain neglected like foster children. Just consider the utopian chatter being spread about vision. Many things which can be achieved by small improvements are lost in the overall vision. In the thin air of the future the danger is real that the concrete demands of the present will be devalued as unimportant details. More to the point: the mega plans frequently permit companies to cling to their internal incompetencies. Often it can be said: *Those who need a vision have nothing to offer at present.*

By focussing on targets the future is prioritized at the expense of the present. A concrete example of this: one large concern in the food industry made gold rush profits after the re-unification of Germany in 1989 and they raised the expectations of the American parent company correspondingly for the following years as well. Recession and other influences meant that these expectations were not met; growth was only slight and again one of those self-staged dramas was produced which were based on the expectations which had been set far too high, and are common in top-down cultures. On record is how one manager, during a meeting, roared quite sincerely at a laughing employee: »What are you laughing about! You apparently have not grasped the seriousness of the situation.« The belief is still widespread that dogged efforts and an atmosphere of long faces can release something called »additional« motivation. This is precisely the way to miss the target. For the gods have given fun priority over success.

Another phenomenon which you are probably familiar with: »Once I have reached this goal, then I will …« – »After the next promotion I'll be satisfied, then I can ...« This is how the pupil thinks about exams, the student about his finals, the trainee about the appointment to the Board and the Board Member about »retirement« and cultivating his hobbies. Many people, unconcerned about the riches surrounding them, seem to be standing on their toes to get a glimpse of what the future may bring. Enjoy my work *now*? Later! Later!

This is also an experience that many have made: the strange emptiness, once the goal is reached. Reaching a goal means: looking for a new one. Further! Further! A goal – as a goal – is something which, in fact, you can only *destroy*. Received wisdom says: People who have goals should be careful not to achieve them. Up for the next round! Sisyphus's failure was not the hopelessness of his efforts; it was simply the illusion, he would be happy if he reached his goal: if the stone stayed on top of the hill.

Carpe diem

The prerequisite for excellence is the joy in the doing.

Whoever only has the goal in his head freezes up. That has consequences for commitment. May I cite one of the greatest sources of quotations? »The spirit neither looks forward, nor backward. Only the present is the source of our happiness.« These lines from Goethe's *Faust II* describe a concentration on the present moment, which appears primarily in the Epicureans' experience of time in antiquity. The stuff of archives? For commitment, it is practical to argue that, that, strictly speaking, only the indeterminate present can be experienced. The moment is the only point of contact with reality, indeed, it *is* the whole of reality. The past is past, and the future will never be part of the individual's conscious experience. Future events, when they are experienced, are always in the present. Tomorrow never comes. But those who have never learned to concentrate their energies on the here and now will not really consciously experience this later present either.

»The intention of making people happy is not part of the plan of creation.« These words by a resigned Sigmund Freud can only be seconded if you understand happiness as an aim. Since Aristotle we know a second, more practical notion of happiness: the happiness of the *traveler*. The happy person does not look towards the future. He is full of energy *now*. Involvement does not think of tomorrow. The »carpe diem« of Horaz, who in Peter Weir's film »Dead Poet Society« experienced an unexpected renaissance, views this uniqueness of the moment as a prerequisite for commitment. The ancient Greeks knew that you can never be happy if you are not happy at the moment. Now or never! Moreover, you do not need anything else to be happy than *wanting* to be happy. Past and future cannot contribute anything. An American proverb says: »Life is what happens to you while you're busy making other plans.«

Driven out of the working day: concentration on concentration, immersion in immersion, being grounded in meditation, working on inner peace, a leisurely pace, and taking things easy – all of this has been banned to the ghettos of management seminars (and is frequently used there as rational cosmetics for proceeding as usual). It is instrumentalized to intensify a forward rushing, aggressively active and target-oriented self-igniting dynamism. But highly-concentrated interest in the business at hand is particularly important for the creativity which companies desperately want. The sort of interest which focuses energies like a parabolic mirror and without which the qualitative leap of innovative re-combining is not possible.

But just as many people wait for a better tomorrow (whatever that may look like: waiting to knock-off, for the weekend, for vacation, promotion, retirement; »once I have …«), similarly most corporate cultures are grounded in *preparing*. The company as a take-off and landing runway. A waiting room. You have barely touched down and already you are taking off again. The flight doesn't count. We deplace ourselves as Paul Virilo said. Travel? Transport! Working to achieve goals. Work conceived as a count-down. A breathless, huffing and puffing, mobilization, because they constantly look into the future, blind to the present. In this mediated reality of the »in order to« the joy of being here and the value of now both disappear.

Real travelers have no goal, only direction. They do not go somewhere, they constantly discover that they are somewhere else. They do not travel to *cover* distance but to *discover* distance. It is not the goal which makes the journey necessary, but the journey which makes the goal possible. The Austrian psychologist Viktor Frankl – a surviving witness of the Nazi concentration camps – summarizes the situation as follows: »Do not aim for a success – the more you put into it and declare it to be your goal the more likely it is you will fall short. Success, like happiness, cannot be pursued; it must result as an unintended by-product, when people devote themselves to something.« Kaizen. »Kai« is the »good«. »Zen« is the »path«. This cannot be repeated often enough to fundamentalist cost-cutters: without zen, no kaizen.

Agreed: As in every other case, here too the danger exists of dashing into the arms of a misunderstanding. A complete renunciation of goals would imply withdrawal behind the walls of a monastery. Goals support orientation and give direction to activities. Shared goals bundle energies, and executives need to look ahead, to avoid danger and to secure the survival of the company over the long term. No question about it: acting responsibly also means seeing where we are going.

Having expectations for the future, however, does not mean that the goal justifies the path. On the contrary, the path justifies the goal. Commitment too does not come so much from goals or future plans, but from the personal experience of the shared path. This requires interaction, credibility, community. K. Weick was able to show – in complete contradiction to commonly held corporate concepts – that a common goal definition by no means instigates cooperation between people, but the common path. The goal idea is based on the presumption that it is possible to implant, so to speak, a goal idea into people from outside. All employees in a business pursue, no matter what they do, their own, »inner« defined values, standards, goals. What ties all of them together is the path. This common path is the company: the playing field on which these values are applied. Play to end the game? Play for the sake of playing!

More importantly this also impacts concretely on how work at the company is experienced: It may be that the top executives are permanently busy with goals. Across the bottom of the corporate pyramid goals hardly play a role. What people experience is the »how«, the mood, the atmosphere, everything which is part of the path. Employees only deal with goals for a tiny fraction of their working time. That is not a bad idea: Those who stick permanently to goals are nowhere. When I examine how much energy is invested at management level in finding and »implementing« goals and how much attention is paid to the experienced, down-to-earth »how«, then the wisdom of the procedure is questionable.

The problem does not arise, therefore, until people are so rigidly sticking to the goal that they no longer experience joy on the path of the present. Ralph Waldo Emerson: »We are always standing on the threshold of life.« Commitment means: discovering reward in the event at the moment. What is meant is the ability of directing one's attention to a task, concentrating, and not letting oneself be distracted.

In this context I am concerned with concentrating energy in situative experience. People who only experience happiness and satisfaction when they reach goals, people who pursue a goal compulsively – they do not have all their energy available for the here and now in their work. Some of their energy is always elsewhere, in tomorrow. (Our parent's generation used to call this »saving for a rainy day.«) They do not do something for its own sake but because they want to do something else later: people who live according to the grammar of re-sale value. Their present is a »not yet« condition, and correspondingly deficient – and this is precisely the reason for their halfhearted actions, less than optimal results and finally, missed targets. They never arrive, because they are never in their own present. They always have an alibi – a word which means »somewhere else«. So they are, once again, not responsible, because they are not »responsive« *now*. Oliver Cromwell is supposed to have said: »A man never climbs higher than when he does not know where he is going to.«

Thus, concentrating energy in the present does not mean living completely for the moment. Action in anticipation of what is coming should only be moderated to the point where the present is not devalued and we do not let ourselves be distracted or shook up. Everything that frightens us is in view of the future. But we can only act now.

The joy in immediate experience drives individuals to creativity and extraordinary achievements. This pleasure is dependent on focussing energy. The tennis player Pete Sampras, when asked what his secret for success was: »I never try to win a tournament. Nor do I try to win a set or a game. I only want to win this one point.« Or, closer to day-to-day business life, Edgar Thoms, one of the most successful district managers of Provinzial insurance:

»I never think about the annual premium, the monthly report or the quarterly results. I only think of this customer who is sitting right in front of me and who, at this time, is the most important discussion partner in my life.« Any other attitude weakens your position.

Several years ago I had the opportunity to spend several weeks with Hopi Indians. One afternoon I took over the job of peeling potatoes for the whole extended family. I could not have looked especially happy at the prospect – anyway, an elderly Hopi woman, bending over me, pointed to the potato and knife in my hands and said: »Get into it.«

Decisiveness

As cultural complexity increases, so do the number of choices, but this is often by no means experienced as available freedom but rather as insecurity, as inner conflict in the face of the wide scope of interactive possibilities, even as a source of numbing absence of orientation. The apples in the neighbor's garden ... real life takes place elsewhere ..., why not do something completely different ..., at the next job everything will be different ... – there are so many interests which are competing in the inner monologue that it is difficult to set clear priorities. The more options, the more important is decisiveness – anyone who has zapped through the various TV channels for an evening knows the unsatisfactory feeling of insufficient decisiveness.

It is helpful to ask yourself from time to time: What do I *really* want to do? Am I on the right playing field? Am I making a genuine contribution? Do I make a difference by performing my work? An employee of a mid-sized textile manufacturer who, voluntarily, dropped his managerial tasks and, by so doing, ran into lack of understanding on the part of some colleagues, but private support from many, describes his dilemma and his choice: »I had a great position, a very cooperative boss, really nice and skilled employees. I was well paid and was even assured a promotion. But as time went by I noticed that I was missing something: the calm and concentrated work on technical problems, working out system solutions, which is what I had studied. There was no time left for that, and it became clear to me, that that was most important. Frequently I tried to tell myself how great my work was. But at some time or another I just made up my mind: against the management role and for my own interest.«

My interest – it is the decisiveness which makes the difference. This manager felt that the management role or even the promotion causes more stress than it is really worth. Whatever may be important to one person, whatever another may feel, is completely unimportant: »I decided, that is the way to go.« This is the formula which clarifies the inner confusion of demands and the inner conflict in favor of clear priorities. It is important to know that we have chosen our path ourselves and that our happiness is in our hands. Without choosing, wanting is aimless, without wanting, choosing is powerless.

When all one's energy stands behind a decision – who could deny that this is the royal road to success? Negatively seen: The only reason why you are possibly not successful in this work is that you do not perform it with love and devotion. Instead, you do it to please your boss, to rise one more step in your career, to book the next holiday, to rest on the lotus blossom of retirement, to meet the expectations of your parents and friends, to make the highway of your marital boredom somewhat more bearable, to ... means to an end ..., later! Later!

Workaholics

That should not be confused with workaholism. Workaholics do not consciously choose work. Work chooses them. They are also not responsible – because the value they attach to their work is unquestioning, supra-individual and, therefore, totalitarian.

The cheery relaxed attitude as a synthesis of depression and excitement is foreign to them. They work compulsively. As a rule, in order to avoid something. They work as a substitute, in order not to have to face up to another, pressing problem. As always, the truth here is: The ability of people to put up with annoyances is greater then their readiness to get rid of annoyances. These people remain passive, because they avoid the things that need doing; and they are dependent, because they need the drug of work to distract themselves – but they do not really choose, as part of a conscious decision-making process, to reject the alternative possibility. It is a mistake to believe that such operative activism could result in something good for the company. Although, perhaps one should respect the voluntary self-destructiveness inside the workaholic.

In business magazine you can read over and over again about captains of industry who work an 80 hour week. In a grotesque form of self-castration they declare proudly that they have not had hardly any time to take vacation in recent years. Respectful faces all around. Impressed by so much vainly staged importance. But it is often more smoke than fire. I know managers who believe they can gauge the commitment of their employees by their overtime or their readiness to work on the weekend. If you leave aside the early industrial orientation (lat. »industria« = hardworking) on purely quantitative yardsticks, then my experience tells me something else: By far the best managers which I have met lead a balanced life. A life, in which recreation also played an important role, taking the fact into consideration that they also want to continue doing a good job for their companies in fifteen years. The attendance list is not a yardstick for commitment.

Commitment also includes being able to allow your energy to fluctuate. Like all power voltage, our life energy fluctuates from time to time. Nobody can work for eight hours a day, continuously, at the same highly concentrated level of performance. The occasional absence of enthusiasm is also part of commitment. It is important to recognize this as being human (something which today we find difficult to say without a condescending tone of voice). A long drop in our energy level is even a useful warning signal, possibly a signal of approaching changes. There is a creative attitude towards life which accepts the energetic ups and downs of life and does not want to pervert it into an eternal up. That too is commitment: being aware of yourself, alert, feeling what is going on inside, recognizing when burdens are too great and learning how to deal with them, not ignoring signs of exhaustion. Only those who can completely break from work, can get completely into it. What destroys people, is tepidness.

Willpower

L. H. Farber in his inspiring book »The Ways of the Will« described the will as the genuinely »responsible mover«. For Rollo May there is a close connection between will and identity: »›I‹ is the ›I‹ of the ›I can‹, … ›I can‹ and ›I will‹ are the essential experience of identity.« But if self-actualization is talked about, what is often meant is a tangled mix of hedonism and craving for success. True self-actualization, however, is substituting »I should« with »I want to«.

Commitment on the job then means: I can because I know what I want. The work is not only done, it is wanted. *We must want to do what we do.*

All work is a self-portrait signed by you.

Responding

The way you are is the way the company is.

The subject of this chapter can be best illustrated by a story, a cave parable, which was told somewhat differently by Bernard Benson, some 2300 years after Plato.

A youngster, thirsty for knowledge, once sought out an elderly hermit who – it was said – knew the answer to any question. »I would like to know: What is right and wrong, lovely and ugly, good and evil?« The old man stared for a while into the flames of his fire. »Behind me is the entrance to a cave«, he answered finally, »there you can go in and find the truth. Take this lantern and you will see it.«

Curious, the youngster went into the cave. It appeared to him completely gray, cold and haunted. The further he went the darker the shadows moving across the wall became. Finally he stopped and said to himself: »That cannot be. There must be very beautiful things to see in this cave.«

Then he suddenly discovered small pools in the stone, water falls, crystals, colors. »That is my light!« he thought. »What I see around me depends solely on me.« Excited he ran back out of the cave. There he found the old hermit again and asked him: »What color are the cave walls really?«

The old man's eyes became dull and expressionless, and he fell into a deep silence.

In daily experience there is no doubt that we perceive the world through our senses as it really is and that it is the way we perceive it. If this were not so, how would we have been able to survive so long? But for some people the question of where water comes from is answered by the existence of water faucets. Researchers in biology and neurophysiology such as Heinz von Foerster, Ernst von Glasersfeld, Fransisco Varela or Gerhard Roth, now tell us that, due to the way our brain works, we do not take in reality by a process of recognition, but on the contrary, *by constructing it ourselves*. We »create it«, so to speak, by adding an inner layer to the external stimulus.

Many insights, arrived at by scientists since antiquity, point us in this direction:

»We can only compare our perception with our perceptions, never with the object of our perception (…)« (Sextus Empiricus, 3rd century A. D.).

»The assumption of an external world will always remain a matter of belief since what we know of it, we know indeed only as inner knowledge (…)« (G. Th. Fechner, 1879).

»This is the strongest type of alienation: our blindness to a world of relative truths which we create ourselves and for which, therefore, the only absolute point of reference is the individual person (…)« (H. Maturana, 1982).

These are doubtlessly difficult thoughts to digest for our supposedly »healthy« common sense. It assumes that we perceive reality »out there« by our senses and recognize it with ever greater precision, step by step. But we also wrongly believe that an illuminated object lights up – although it only reflects.

Perception and recognition should not be understood so much as reproducing reality, but as activities which »create« reality.

Grasping reality is thus action and not reaction. »We respond« – I do not believe that 3M Germany knows what a treasure their slogan is.

»Click-Clack« – The language of our brain

Our senses are not passive organs, but active abilities. We do not see with our eyes: we see with our brain. We do not hear with our ears: we hear with our memory. We add something to the objects and events of our surroundings, and the combined result is what we call reality.

You can experience this yourself at this moment: While you are reading this book, in your head a continuous »click«, »clack«, »click«, »clack« is taking place. Translated this means: »Now he is right«, »No, that is wrong«, »Now he is right again«, »No, that is completely off the wall.« Generally this is called »thinking«. Our understanding tends to react reflexively to everything which does not correspond to our own experience, by saying it is wrong, and to agree with arguments which our experience confirms. We translate the events around us into our own »language« and attach a significance to it supported by our experience. The »original« is irrevocably lost. We can take it for granted that these surroundings, the »original«, continues to exist if we or any other person exists to interpret events. But this assumption of an objectively existing world is neither compulsory nor important for our interests. We can argue that it exists – but that is the only thing that we can say about it.

So anyone who warns you not to loose sight of reality does not realize that it also exists where Cassandra did not suppose it to be.

Faulty perception?

It is the observer who generates the image of reality. Roland Barthes, in another context, considered the birth of the reader as being the equivalent of the death of the author. The absolute is illusory, the finiteness of meaning would be the end of freedom: we are free in how we experience something; nobody forces meaning on us. Emerson writes in his grandiose essay »Self-confidence«: »The painting is waiting for my judgement; it is not called upon to control me, but rather I am the agent who can determine its claims to recognition.« The world is not a uni-verse but rather a multiverse.

So it makes no sense to talk about a »distorted« sense of reality. Nor is there any such thing as »errors« of perception, as communication psychologists would like to have us believe. Perception is construction and interpretation. (Anyone who has suffered the painful experience of having their Literature papers graded can confirm this.) Truth is a question of *individual perspectives*, the allocation of meaning. Furthermore, perspectives are as different as snow flakes.

Again: our »response« to events and phenomena in our surroundings is influenced in distinctly different ways by our experience. What you perceive you accept as true. You cannot perceive something »wrongly«. It is only other people who always maintain that you do not look at things in the right way. But whatever you say:

You are right. The catch is: the others are right, too.

What good is this idea for my daily work at the company? A lot! If we take this perspective seriously the consequence for the company is a revolutionary re-orientation. The question is: what does a company look like if the decisive thought categories are not truth and objectivity, but rather relevance and usefulness?

The company in the mind

The world is always in your mind. This is not only dependent on our experience but also on our interests, which control our attentiveness. If you have just bought a specific car in a specific color, suddenly all the streets are full of this one car in this one color.

The company, too, is always the company in your mind. So it may appear to every manager what a company »is« and how it is different from other organizations. But it is also indisputable that each manager »sees« another company, considers different things important and, in this way, »constructs their own« company according to perspective. The company is the way you *experience* it. It is a projection of your inner world. Each individual maps the company out in a different way. But this map should not be confused with the company itself. For there »is« really no company at all. Only in the minds of the participants.

Heinz Pechek, director of the Austrian Centre for Productivity and Economy: »Entrepreneurs say again and again, that they want ›involved, committed, employees with a business mind-set.‹ Frequently what entrepreneurs mean by that is, the others must think like they do. They expect employees to think, decide and act like they do, ›like entrepreneurs‹. That cannot be realized in practice, because everyone sees things from their own perspective.«

Another example: The organizational chart of a company may show who the boss is and who the subordinates are. But it does not say anything at all about what is really important for the individuals and, thus, for the success of the company: Who talks with whom when solving daily problems (consultant network); who has confidential discussions with whom and exchanges delicate business policy information (confidence network); who gladly and successfully cooperates with whom (cooperation network). These hidden structures behind the official organizational plan – D. Krackhardt and J. Hanson described them – are informal networks which are not set down anywhere but which are *experienced* by the employees and which, therefore, have a decisive effect on productivity and organizational structure.

You, as an observer, are constantly differentiating, by connecting, in your mind, certain types of behavior and placing them in certain categories. If you think as a manager of your staff as a group, a system is created in your mind. Perhaps you differentiate between the »good« and the »bad« employees, between »foot-draggers« and »go-getters«, perhaps between »young« and »old«, between men and women, between specialists and generalists. These differences depend on your values and interests. The image in your mind will be different depending on what you consider important. Not one of them is better or worse, at most one may be more practical and relevant for certain purposes.

Or: leadership can perform miracles. Due to a promotion the subordinate suddenly, as if by magic, has become a »supervisor«. The business sociologist Goetz Briefs already wrote in 1931 that promotion to a supervisory position can make strangers out of good acquaintances who are then compelled to work together as if they were acquaintances. The promoted individual may feel the same as before, and may experience the same collegial relationship as before. But this does not work: the former colleagues now *experience* them differently. A new person has emerged. Where once two colleagues shared the same cafeteria table,– hocus-pocus! – there is suddenly a boss and a subordinate. The discussion runs differently, facial expressions and gestures change; suddenly there are issues which they do not talk about anymore. In the brain of the newly »created« *subordinate*, besides the film »What do I want to say?« is the additional film »How is she assessing me now?« The boss, in addition to the videotape of the actual subject of discussion, is sensing »Does she want to impress me?« or »Is he a good employee?« Paraphrasing a well-known formula as stated by Watzlawick: *Not leading is not possible*. Everything is understood as an announcement or a challenge. In a coaching situation a business unit supervisor told me: »Barely do I start to think out loud than all the wheels start turning and people consider what I have said to be an instruction.«

A lesson: Not until I left 3M many years ago had I understood that my chief executive, whose corporate management I frequently disagreed with, worked in a completely different company than I did. Oh yes, we both received our money from the same payroll office. But when *he* thought about the company, when *he* prepared to make decisions, when *he* spoke about internal company processes, then he had completely different images in his mind. He heard completely different voices which whispered to him as he made decisions, he had other experiences, other people to speak to, other interests, other sets of values. The great leveler called conformity to corporate culture cannot erase that. The larger a company is the more incomprehensible the top-down decisions are. Not because »those at the top« are mentally handicapped. But because they live in another reality. Briefly: We do not all work in the same company.

Looked at this way, every person, at all times and in all situations, acts in an economically rational manner. Their behavior is sensible. It makes sense. From their perspective. But there is no other yardstick than »individual perspective«, although another may secretly claim to have »better« access to the truth, to »objective« criteria. For this reason a type of behavior, from the point of view of an observer, no matter how »ludicrous« it may appear, is sensible from the inner perspective. It helps little (»That's crazy!) to try to argue with them. From their point of view each individual *always* acts rationally and economically.

Five point seven, five point six, five point nine

The same applies to assessments: »The subject has nothing to do with anything outside of yourself, but only about you, yourself« (Johann Gottlieb Fichte). I would like to treat this subject in greater depth at a later point, but for now only this: assessments illustrate primarily the characteristics and perspectives of the person who passes judgement, not the judged. If you seek the reality about another person, you will never find anything but yourself. You discover, for example, not the employee, »as he really is« but as you have *created* him. Any assessment says, therefore, more about the evaluator than the person evaluated.

For each person evaluates the activity of another (service or a product) according to an individual value system. What a product is cannot be determined by the seller. It is determined by the buyer. In the internal relationship between manager and employee as well: you think perhaps you have done the employee a service, but the employee does not recognize this service at all. Due to other values. You are angry about the lack of gratitude; the employee is confused about your direct or indirect demands for a quid pro quo.

This is the radical autonomy of allocating values: whether a service is really a service is decided exclusively by the buyer. There is no objective yardstick for a product. The observation has been repeatedly made that some administrative department or another provides services which nobody in particular wants. So there is therefore no extrinsic (from without) motivation either. All motivation is intrinsic (from within), for it corresponds to an inward, individual allocation of value of what is to be performed or neglected.

The realm of freedom

Thus, organization is an event which takes place in the minds of those participating, and nowhere else.

People are also, in this respect, not recipients of impressions, but creators of expressions. This places the accent on individual activity instead of outward control and mere governing: »The essence of truth is revealed as freedom« (Martin Heidegger). The outward world in the company holds all – really all – options open, and it is by no means the case that it compels you to experience it, they way you experience it. *You are completely responsible for your response.*

Moreover, how you respond depends on your inward disposition. How often, for example, can an employee fail to perceive something which a colleague takes practically for granted. Or when conflicts arise: Many fantasize about other people's motives and create a »Menu: Conflicts«. The motto: »The other is harboring a grudge against me.« Then they eat the menu instead of the food, finally complaining about how badly it tasted and feel that their suspicion that someone wanted to poison them, has been confirmed. The drama is always a drama in their heads.

If you want to tie your dissatisfaction to the company you have forgotten that initially only your »response« to the events in the company and not the company itself is defective. Even if it is sometimes difficult to see through it: it is the individuals who create the company. That means: the company is an example of how you describe yourself. Mirror, mirror ... You are wasting your time and energy, if you blame someone or something »out there«. You do not see the company as *it* is but as *you* are. But whichever view you choose depends on what you are like.

Acting responsibly then means responding appropriately to a situation. Are you exposed to the power of routine, conditioned reflexes, imprisoned in the armament of genes, victim of existential programs which were inscribed in your cerebral cortex? Not at all. You can choose the response. You can change your attitude towards things. That does not mean that you should deny the facts of the matter. It does mean that you assume responsibility for *how* you *experience* it, which perspective you choose. That you recognize your own contribution to this reality. A sensible, a very helpful question: »What am I contributing to this experience?« And: »What does this company say about me as a person?«

Between the stimulus from your surroundings and the way you react is the empire of freedom: to be responsible for your response. You *decide* in favor of suffering, being unhappy, letting yourself be disparaged, cultivating a feeling of being victimized, permitting others to have power over you. Or you decide for another kind of response: assuming responsibility, living commitment. Commitment for a situation is then, and only then, possible, if you experience yourself as a participant. As a co-worker. »To be committed« does not release you from all your professional and private problems. But control is moved from others to within yourself. In this way you make yourself responsible for your experience.

Let us take »stress« as an example, for which many seminars offer lots of preventative and curative remedies. I would not hesitate a moment simply to disqualify all of these as sophisticated nonsense (mind machines!) if the false assumption were not widespread that, in fact, such a thing as stress exists. Stress does not exist as such, but is created by individuals under certain circumstances because they have chosen this experience. Some people remain cool and collected even when five telephones are ringing at the same time, and work at their best when such situations arise. Some lose their temper. Who is responsible? The telephones?

Nothing and nobody can stress you. All individuals create stress against the backdrop of their own personal experience. They give things their individual importance, they import meaning to them. They are eminently creative because they actively shape their experience. And what irritates some people no end, does not bother others one bit.

Don't lose my temper

»My boss annoyed me.« Is that possible? Of course not. You produce your own anger, because you have chosen to get angry. Due to your belief that, in respect to your own value system, this is the appropriate reaction. Nothing and nobody can get you angry. You have to allow them to. The game, called Parcheesi in America, is called »Don't lose your temper!« in Germany, not »Don't lose my temper!«

However, there is a general tendency to blame the company, the boss, the colleagues, the employees: »This boss is really ineffectual and incompetent.« But the boss is not like that. *You* make him like that. You are the person feeling the discomfort; you can also change this. Do not wait for others to do something, you may have to wait a long time for that to happen. As the others experience the situation differently.

Anger about an employee starts from the wish: »If you were only more similar to me.« But the employee is not like that. Many people have a terribly hard time, granting other people the right to be different than their expectations of them. Any anger is the result of compulsive expectations. Once we recognize that we are not free of our problems but we are free of the paralysis they can cause.

Of course: people who lose their tempers attract attention, feel important and are always on the right side. »It is a matter of fact!« But it never was a matter of fact. Each party may think they are disputing »the facts of the case« based on the most general principles of how »you« should behave. But what they are doing is merely making their own standards, experiences and views obligatory for all the others. What right do they have to do this?

Feelings

It is not the events themselves that hurt us. It is how we react to them. But can we also chose this reaction? *Do we decide* to be unhappy? I hear the objection that this is all thought out much too rationally. Feelings are involved here, and feelings can frequently »overwhelm« people. Is it possible to control feelings at all?

Way back in the cozy cultures of the '68 generation calling upon feelings was a way people had of immunizing themselves against any and all reasonable examinations of rational approaches to living. »It's just my feeling...« and the discussion was over. Feelings were accorded the greatest respect. Even today it is common to excuse certain forms of behavior by feelings. A short list of linguistic carelessness:

»He and his perfectionism drive me absolutely nuts.«
»I can't help feeling this way.«
»When you said that we had lost control over the project, you really upset me.«
»You made me feel ashamed in front of the whole staff.«
»Do I look wasted? We are right in the middle of our annual report; you can imagine what is going on here.«

All these sentences have a hidden meaning: »I am not responsible for my reaction. The others, or the circumstances compel me to feel this way.« Try a short exercise. The next time you have a discussion, pay attention to how much time is used up for tales of woe, complaints, whingeing and hopeless cases: You will be surprised how much time accumulates; and how much irresponsibility.

The separation of thinking from feeling, which is so widespread in our culture, stands on thin ice. We cannot feel, without thinking, and we cannot think, without feeling at the same time. Corresponding to our experience in the past we produce directed emotional energies, which supply our thoughts with energy and which we then sense as feelings. Thoughts influence feelings. Feelings, in turn, influence thoughts.

The separation between »mind« and »heart« may be popular, but it is not sustainable. It would mean the end of human freedom. Why so popular? Because it seems to relieve us of responsibility. We draw attention to the independent dynamic of our emotions and hope for a discount price. The files of the traffic police are full of reports from the valley of tears. »When somebody drives so badly, you *have to* lose your temper!«

Feelings, in the end, are the creations of our past experience for the purpose of establishing that we are right. The issue is not to suppress them. But we are just as responsible for our feelings as we are for our thoughts. Both are closely related. There is no difference between the preceding rational »recognition« and the subsequent emotional »interpretation«. That is why we can influence our feelings, by changing the quality of our consciousness, our thoughts. By responding in *a different* way.

Please examine this thought carefully first, before you reject it. It may be helpful to imagine that you certainly have responded frequently by a spontaneous show of feelings. But soon after you can – if you want to – step aside in your mind, observe your behavior, and decide whether you want to continue responding in this way. It is simply practical to think this way: nobody is so important that he is worth getting upset about.

I remember very well a young manager, who was disturbed by the fact that her boss obviously had very little confidence in her and, when a difficult matter arose, frequently gave other employees preference – until it became clear to her that she herself was the person who had allowed this fact to become so important to her. That she gave it significance. She allowed this boss to have an extraordinary amount of influence on the quality of her life (to the point of sleepless nights) and permitted his judgement to damage her own sense of self-worth. She attached more importance to someone else's thoughts than to her own. She began to believe it was a »true« judgement about her. She transfered the responsibility for her feelings to the boss. But nobody forced her to feel this way. It was up to her simply to refuse to accept this situation, and to change it: to describe her situation, to compare it with her boss's view and to renegotiate the situation. Or to vote with her feet.

The phrase »individual responsibility« reflects the fact that we respond. We are responsible, capable of responding to our own selves. *That* is the authority to which responsibility is a fact. Many – as a knee-jerk reaction – let themselves be controlled by what others think is right or wrong. Anyone who becomes aware of their responsibility for their experience, experiences themselves as shapers of their own lives. They empower themselves. That is the basic prerequisite for excellence: if you are responsible to yourself for what you do; if you do not care – at least to a certain extent – what others think about it. Otherwise you make yourself dependent on the whim of a thumbs-up or thumbs-down.

Know thyself!

»For they know not what they do.« Most executives really are not aware of the fact that it is not the »objective facts« but their view of the world, their inward reference system, which is expressed in objects. That is why they are not interested in themselves, and even less in the uniqueness of their experience. They are primarily interested in what takes place in the periphery of their existence, without recognizing that something is taking place *inside themselves*.

When the management guru Peter F. Drucker, then well beyond the age of 80, was asked in an interview in early 1993 what tip he could give to young executives based on his many years of experience, his response was »Know yourself!« Some who were looking for the »golden rule«, the trick to top all tricks, may have been disappointed. But, against the backdrop of the discussion up to this point, it is undeniable how important to responsible leadership this »gnothi seauton!« is, which was once chiseled into the stone over the entrance of the Apollo Temple at Delphi. »Choosing a response« presumes that one knows the directing factors of one's own personality, the individual earmarks and role images: What determines the film script of my life? What are the most important images of good and poor leadership, right and wrong, which I bear within me, some since early childhood? What makes me tick? Where am I sensitive?

Only if you yourself look at the essential motivations for your activity, the »articles of faith« in your life, can you distance yourself from them, i. e. can you cease acting automatically. Otherwise you merely restore your inner museum. It looks like self-determination. But it is in fact extremely other-directed. You can modify your decision at any time, pick new articles of belief or add to them. For leadership this is absolutely necessary: *Only people who have encountered themselves can encounter others.* »I know who I was, who I am and who I want to be,« says Dan Kaplan, the President of the Hertz Equipment Rental Corporation, »in other words: I know the extent of commitment that I am prepared to enter, and I know *why* I am prepared to enter it.« Here, too, the observation applies:

People who are aware of themselves go further.

That also applies to the film script of your individual life: your past – it does not *exist*. It is a fiction. It only exists in your head. You tell yourself and others stories about it. (That is why God envies historians: they can continually rewrite history.) You have decided to judge certain matters in this way, and not in another. Often to pre-judge. You are responsible for this interpretation. You can see things this way. But you do not have to see things like this. It is never too late for a happy childhood.

»The key to successful leadership is self-awareness,« writes James Autry, chief executive of an American magazine publisher, and this statement – which has always been true – is receiving an additional boost by the rapid globalization of the economy. Key word: multicultural competence. The mere fact of the increasing internationalization of employee composition in businesses (leading: Switzerland – every third employee is a foreigner), the increase in multicultural interfaces, the many international teams: cultural and linguistic hurdles formally compel us to recognize our own values and to respect other value systems. If an »expatriate« looks at his interlocutor through the lenses of his own stereotypes he will – to his own disadvantage – behave inappropriately and unsuccessfully. Thus multicultural competence requires not only deigning tolerance towards a canon of values which otherwise might be considered inferior, but rather curiosity and openness to things new – but also flexibility in respect to one's own values. This means zooming in on personality development instead of lists of ready-made prescriptions. The seminars carried out for the »expats« in the Schweizerischer Bankverein, for example, have repeatedly confirmed the significance of an openness beyond tolerance, especially in the area of »team work«.

Objectively subject

The claim to »objectivity« and »truth« has the same spin as the totalitarianism of the social field experiments of the 20th century. They were founded on mechanical models whose compulsive character robbed the individual of any freedom to act. The individual could not, therefore, assume any responsibility either. It is apparent that such models are irreconcilable with the mental images recommended in this book.

For example, the ethics discussion in and around companies: powered by moralistic feelings, some feel em-powered by their incensed consciences to overpower their reasoning. Anyone who has already been exposed once to the virtue terror of a holy moral indignation knows what I am talking about. Against the aggressive attacks of a self-empowered conscience elite one can only have recourse to the right which also guarantees the freedom to act morally. This right must be respected by both the holy crusaders of moral conviction as well as the representatives of lukewarm, thick-skinned amoralism. Hubert Markl can be applauded when he writes: »More important than being raised to recognize the absolute authority of conscience is being raised to respect our legal system.«

Furthermore »prevailing opinion« does not prove anything either. Nor does so-called »scientific« insight: nothing more than an enormous approximation. »Science does not think,« says Heidegger. What he means by that is, it is based on suppositions which science does not question, but on which it erects its perfectly logical constructions. It is one approach to designing reality rationally, an approach which must be judged by whether it can be followed, and by whether it is useful – and not, by whether it is objective or true.

But all the activity within the company presumes that there are objective facts and yardsticks. That people can arrive at the »truth«. It is in this context that experts intone their Song of Songs – a doubtful cantus when you think how often experts err or merely represent special interest groups. But there are (although I find it difficult to admit this) areas in the company in which the influence of the observer is relatively limited. In these »hard« areas – e.g. whether a machine works or not – unanimity can be achieved relatively easily. Why it may frequently fail to work – that is something more difficult to agree upon. But in the »soft« areas of highly complex social interactions such as markets, teams, employees it is completely misleading to act as if there are objective, hard facts. In the field of human business the perspective of the observer is decisive.

»But look at it objectively!« People who say that are appealing to you (at best) to accept their way of looking at things. They say: »See it the way I do it!« But that is impossible. »Objectively« translated means: prior to any experience. But there is nothing there for people to grasp.

Such an »informed« perspective has enormous consequences for executive officers in companies. Leadership positions in most of German industry still largely call for specialized background in some field of knowledge. In many corporate business units this expertise is usually in one of the natural sciences. I do not want to step on the toes of any chemists at BASF, Bayer or Hoechst, and there are also many executive officers who have been blessed with the best combination of scientific expertise and social skills. But the tendency is: it is no accident that these chemists studied what they studied.

There are certainly many exceptions. But my experience has taught me that natural scientists in particular, due to their education and the worlds they live in, tend to have great difficulty recognizing the subjective nature of what is called »reality«. For them things tend to be beyond a shadow of a doubt, »objective«, so to speak. If you confront a manager, for example, with the alternative of either dealing with detailed engineering questions or with matters involving personnel, given the same salary and the same prestige, three out of four executive officers will prefer the engineering tasks. Fritz B. Simon recognizes in this »a sheer boundless yearning for the calculable functioning and reliability of trivial machines. The hard reality of factual questions where there are clear data and formulas, to find out what is ›right‹ and ›wrong‹, promises a simple life, following the rules of logic, where managers know what they have to do.«

»At least figures are objective!« Really? Figures are meaningless. They do not say anything until you start to say them, that means, to use them within a specific context. If someone has achieved 95 percent of his forecast, that only means at first, that he achieved 95 percent of his forecast. A fact. What it means depends on the observer. One may say: »Under the conditions of market turbulence in the past business year to have achieved 95 percent is a great performance. Bravo!« Another says: »5 percent under plan! A catastrophe!« A third: »We must optimize our planning processes.« A fourth: »Planning only substitutes accidents with errors anyway.« Objectively subjective. You are well advised to eliminate the word »objective« from your vocabulary. (Except, perhaps, if you work in the microscope business.)

»But if many other people share the same opinion? That is definitely objective.« The similarity machinery: »I look for people who are like me and they also think this boss is stupid!« Doubtless the feel for the »opinion of others« (what »they« think) usually leads to realistic assessments and sensible behavior. If something sounds plausible, appears credible, is »visible« then we take it to be »true«. But caution is advisable. What we take to be real is namely also highly dependent on other people's perception.

A famous example is an experiment carried out by Solomon E. Asch in which test persons were called upon to compare the lengths of distances. The participants were told to state their opinion loudly and clearly each time. Some of them were instructed in advance unanimously to give the same wrong estimates. The participants then experienced a conflict between their own (accurate) perceptions and the (faulty) perceptions of the other, instructed persons. Result: the test persons began, after a short time, to doubt their own perceptions. Most of them »caved in« and agreed with the (wrong) estimate of the others. Only very few test persons had enough self-confidence to cling to their own opinion to the very end, without expressing substantial uncertainty.

Let us be quite clear about this: even when relatively simple perceptions such as the lengths of lines are at issue, people bow to group pressure. Our own perception is strongly influenced by other people's perception, sometimes even completely undermined. This is naturally highly important for how reality is perceived in business. For plenty of analogous phenomena can be found in companies.

In an example which I experienced myself, the issue at a top management panel discussion was the selection of candidates with high potential for an international development program. I had talked previously with one of the selecting managers about one of the candidates – I'll call him »Ralf Müller« for simplicity's sake. The person I spoke with was absolutely convinced that Ralf Müller »objectively« should be appointed to the high-pot group; his potential was no where near to being fully exploited. In reaction to my questions he intensified his enthusiasm and praised him in the highest possible terms. I had never had any contact with Ralf Müller, and I accepted my partner's description for what it was: a story. If someone tells us a story, he wants to seduce us into accepting his way of looking at things. And this view then justifies his position.

When the management panel took up the subject of Ralf Müller, the chairman of the board was the first to speak: »Ralf Müller, well, I cannot understand at all how his name got added to this group of candidates in the first place. His performance has not been exactly convincing in recent months.« Short silence. Before my former interlocutor could say anything, another member of the board seconded: »I agree completely with your opinion. If Müller is supposed to represent the up-and-coming elite in our company then we have a problem. We have substantially better people.« Nods of agreement all around from the other participants. – My interlocutor did not say anything. Ralf Müller's personnel file was set aside. People have an extremely sensitive antenna for the climate of opinion around them. It is difficult for many, despite having a different opinion, to resist the general trend. If at a meeting an interpretation monopolist has stated an opinion, it sets the ball rolling in a certain direction for the others. If a second, or even a third person agrees, the others become uncertain: they have doubts about their own perception or remain quiet in order not to have to justify themselves or become isolated from the rest of the group. This is how group opinions are formed. Keeping quiet is also a form of communication. The reality created by »quiet spirals« may not be »objective« but its consequences are facts: Ralf Müller is out.

Where that can lead the company can be imagined by anyone who has already seen a company go into bankruptcy: nobody dared to question the favorite program of the chief executive officer.

Creativity

»Creating reality« is the epitome of human freedom. External sensory impulses are only occasions for our inward life. Each external impulse is a new opportunity to choose our in-sight: that this manner of thinking greatly expands the scope for creativity, that without it creativity is in fact not possible, is obvious. For creating means generating, and since we permanently generate our reality, we are permanently creative. Another question is whether we allow ourselves to express and make use of our creativity. I am repeatedly surprised how managers lavish praise on creativity and innovations and, on the other hand, are deaf when it comes to their convictions about the objectivity of »things in themselves«.

Let us look back briefly: a pre-school child walking through the woods feels a sense of belonging to a large organism. The child does not distinguish between itself as subject and the object »woods«. It is in the child. As children we are naturally creative.

Our life is one big adventure playground. We build. Destroy. Build again. We are rich. Rich in innovations. Without limits. Any cardboard box can be our ocean-going liner. We dress up, act out roles and switch from one to another in a matter of seconds when they cease to appeal to us, and we enjoy ourselves in the process.

Under the pressures of growing up this creativity is often buried under conformance to what is generally acceptable. We get our feet on the ground and reach compromises with the apparent objectives of habit and the mapped out path through life. On every subject in life our experience leads us to viewpoints which we then consider right. We are successful and begin to store these successful behavioral patterns and positions.

So, in a certain sense, every experience has a narrowing effect. Convictions are prisons, said Nietzsche. That the German word for »narrowness«, »Enge« has the same root as »Angst«, explains that some people often see the experiences and opinions of others as a downright threat. They become aggressive. They deny other people the right to see things they way they do. They justify themselves, i.e. they »prove themselves right«. Thereby they do nothing more than defend their own past. They continuously »repeat« what they have already experienced, the bottom line of their own biography. »Well, you know, I have 25 years of experience,« one manager told me. In fact, he had only *one* year of managerial experience, and that was 24 years ago.

Being creative means violating the narrowing principles from our past. We can play with the material. We all belong to the family of homo ludens. Thus, being creative means dropping the basic concept that there is one »correct« position on every subject. Curiosity, i.e. eagerness for new experiences, is the core virtue of creativity. Broadening. Permitting oneself to be enriched. This, in turn, means: being able to put »correct« positions and »true« convictions »on hold«. This means that all positions and convictions are in us and cease to be outside of us.

Thus, creativity has the primary characteristic of opening oneself again to go beyond the correct, the necessary or even just the routine. This is the creative re-designing of reality (example: Swatch). The creative power of the individual, the ability, not to copy reality in the learning process, but to create it, is the core of human creativity. Our heads were made round so that thought can change direction, says Francis Picabia. Creativity thus means: Seeing the same thing as all the others. But thinking something different.

If reality in the company is not created by some sort of objective circumstances but by communication, then it can be changed. All change begins in the mind. This is the hour of »creativity« which we are so desperately seeking to uncover in the company. Creativity can be equated with changing the predominant approach to looking at things. Creativity is also *destructive*, in Schumpeter's famous definition: »Innovation is the creative destruction of the existing by entrepreneurs.« For this purpose traditions, conventions, patterns, standards, concepts and roles, briefly: the obligation to follow conventional behavior, must be loosened. That can only work with intensified individuality; that can only work with intensified inner independence; for this purpose the status quo must be disrupted at least somewhat. We have been dreaming the sluggish dreams of solid foundations, objective guarantees and referees for far too long.

By no means do I wish to promote the educated middle class's ideal of individuality. I am referring to the chances offered by subjectivity in recognizing and overcoming problems. That is the skill which is crucial: the ability to switch perspectives. For the subject »quality« nothing is more important. Look at things from inside and outside. Do not assume anything! Do not accept any »thought necessities«! These are Albert Einstein's demands: »Whoever has lost his capacity to be surprised, is, so to speak, dead.«

Robert Nozick pointed out that creative people have, most importantly, *decided* to be creative. One example is the video game giant Sega, whose employees neither punch in and out, nor have any fixed working hours. Hayao Nakayama, the majority shareholder in Sega, consciously turned all the rules of Japanese business on their head in order to create a creative atmosphere. In his office he has framed on display the words of Marcel Proust: »The real voyage of discovery does not consist of searching for new landscapes but in looking at the world with new eyes.« Creativity can only be at home where individuality in companies is explicitly allowed, better still, promoted. The argument of »objectivity«, the mental block which has turned into a compulsive fact: that is the death of innovation.

Given a positive spin: without radical subjectivity there can be no creativity. Companies can decide between the calm of stable conditions and the storm of dynamically creative change. It is simultaneously the decision between not being responsible and the ability to accept assignments. Between convention and change. Between organized irresponsibility and consciously chosen individual responsibility. Boris Pasternak wrote: »The goal of creative activity is to *give oneself*« (emphasis R. S.).

The market is to blame?

How important the quality of our response is to success in business cannot be over-emphasized. The fact, for example, that there are customer complaints, in itself, means nothing. But they are experienced in a variety of ways. If the employees' perspective is, for example: »Complaints are especially unpleasant«, their behavior will be completely different than if they take the view: »Complaints are especially valuable.« In the former case they presumably have defensive strategies in mind and a defensive attitude, to the point where they are aggressive in advance. In the latter case they welcome the complaint as helpful feedback, as market research free of charge and as an invitation to innovate: what a chance to keep the customer when 95 percent of dissatisfied customers simply switch to the competition without saying anything! The customer is the best corporate consultant! If the employees also consider that their own behavior – perhaps incomparably more than any other sensitive post in the company – is the basis of decisions about the image of the company in the surrounding climate of opinion, their inward, mental map can be changed – so that they feel customer anger as a special challenge. They »create« their customers, and they »create« themselves at the same time. From being a victim of circumstances (»I am at the mercy of the customers' attacks«) to being the master of the situation (»I can manage the situation and assure that something useful results for everyone involved«).

We are completely responsible as individuals for how we experience such situations, and what is true for individuals is also true for the whole company. Even if they do not want to see it: The market is to blame! But we can choose in such situations how we experience the outside disruption of balance between the market and the company, and how we react to it. Analyses of the Nixdorf disaster, for example, give a clear impression of mechanical fatalism: It was inevitable. In this way all the responsibility for acting becomes diffused. Similarly, managers frequently attribute the success of their companies to factors which they cannot influence: the right/wrong product at the right/wrong time, the favorable/unfavorable exchange rate of the dollar, economic swings, changes in consumer attitudes. In case of problems, the victimization stories are naturally elaborated: the high personnel costs in Germany, protected foreign markets, the unknown variables of economic policy, subsidized foreign competitors, government regulations, unions, changes in values, society. No generalization is too cheap to avoid a mea culpa. Passion plays. Yet an informal survey of nearly any industry shows: even under the most unfavorable external market conditions, which are identical for everyone, some companies are more successful than others.

There is no direct, compelling cause-effect relationship, as is repeatedly maintained, to explain or even to excuse certain corporate policy decisions (for example, lay-offs). The disruption from outside always leaves many options open. Changes in the markets are never the »cause« for certain effects in the company. They do not »compel« anything. On the contrary, the company has many different options in responding to market fluctuations. This response varies from company to company. Some survive, some do not. They are responsible for the outcome. Never the market.

However small the room for maneuvering may appear – the responsibility of the agent remains, of course, undiminished. The sober cause analysis does not annul in any way the category of personal responsibility. Of course you can, as manager, complain: »Work morale has dropped. The change in values has changed people.« But you can also say: »We are working in structures left over from the 19th century. We have neglected to create a company which people like to work in. How could we change that?« In the former case you are powerless. The victim mind-set pure and simple. In the latter case you assume responsibility: for things as they are and for things as they should be. A question of perspective. Here, too, those who act, have power.

Responsibility of the individual

»The same« situation is open to a large number of interpretations: this way of thinking defines the scope of independence of thought and action which does not bow to any self-styled authority. But it also increases – and this is especially important in this context – the responsibility of individuals for shaping their surroundings. Heinz von Foerster identifies this increase in individual responsibility as the root cause of popular skepticism: »Appealing to objectivity means the same thing as eliminating responsibility; that is why it is so popular.«

»Everything with which we are confronted is only an echo of what we are« (Jean Gebser). *One* answer could be to change things. But you can only do this because you experience it the way you experience it. Do not wait for others to do something. The others experience it differently. When employees wonder that their bosses do not act, remain inactive, do not react: »But they must see it this way too!« They do not. They see it differently, because they are different people. They have different intentions. Their previous background is different. They have different expectations. Only you see it like this. So you are also the person who can tackle it. Only you respond to this situation the way you respond. So you also bear responsibility.

If Nietzsche's statement »Nothing is, how it is« is practical, then the most important task of each individual is to seize the initiative and redefine this »it« again and again. The organization of labor is radically dependent on subjectivity. It must formulate subjective opportunities which consist in recognizing and overcoming disruptions. »But that is subjective!« Yes, namely *because* it is subjective, you are responsible. Individual responsibility can only exist together with radical subjectivity.

Do we understand each other?

In communication and leadership psychology people have been training »active listening« over years. Often less to understand the others any better than to take better advantage of them: »The person who asks the questions leads!« (director's instructions: interested, attentive): »May I ask you a few questions first?«, »So-so«, »Interesting!«, »Hmm, hmm« (sitting face to face, friendly smile, nodding in agreement, head slightly bent forward). Leadership techniques in action. Screw-driver logic. Everything based on the spirit of manipulation.

Then this process was refined. »Empathy« for example was now required. People should be sympathetically inclined to the employee. You act responsibly if you recognize your outer world as a mirror image of your inner world: try to see it once through his eyes. Somehow sounded nice. But it had a reverse side, it was always slightly condescending, from the position of a dispensing, higher authority (for transactional analysts: a camouflaged version of the good parent). The unequal communication between two people, one the researcher and the other, the object of research.

It does not work. Because it cannot work. Not because it is ideologically or power-based. In dry terms – because neuropsychology informs us:

Understanding is unlikely.

In the beginning was the word. Immediately thereafter came the misunderstanding. Our language signals may usually suffice for mutual cooperation. We are even capable of impressive cooperative achievements. But, in the end, we will never understand the other person. We will never know how he experiences us. We will never know what his inward image looks like when we both believe we are talking about the same subject. Even if you work for twenty years with your colleague: you do not have an inkling how he or she experiences *you*.

That understanding is improbable is reflected in the etymology of the German word for understanding »verstehen« which can be separated into »ver« (for) and »stehen« (stand), or standing for someone, or in someone else's place. Looked at in physical terms this is an impossibility: Nobody else can stand exactly on the same spot, at the same time, as someone else. Not understanding, looked at this way, is the normal state of affairs.

We may be able to exchange the counterfeit coins of our language characters. But these too would be interpreted again differently, and a different significance would be attached. Theodor W. Adorno wrote: »I try to express what I recognize and what I think. But I cannot do so in accordance with what people will get out of it, or what will become of it.« It is even very probable that we say the most important things only to ourselves, and in a dialect which only we understand. Once, when Robert Schumann was asked to explain a difficult étude, he played it a second time.

The only account we can give regarding an encounter of two free agents is an intuitive one. We believe we have understood the other. Indeed, this belief is also sufficient for normal cooperation in business. Looked at from this perspective it is really a miracle that cooperation generally works so well. But it also explains the existence of an undeniable portion of incomprehension which is decisive, especially when social interaction is emotionally charged.

It is therefore nonsense, as is currently still being done, to talk about »poor communication«. Behind this phrase is the idea of »perfect communication«, which would be the equivalent of congruent inward maps, and a staff made up of people all cloned from the same individual. Misunderstandings are also unavoidable no matter how ideal communicative behavior may be. They are the general rule, not the exception.

But does not »talking to each other« communicate what people have in common? It is considered the basis of community and teams in the company. But it is the opposite: a wolf in sheep's clothing. If people grasp messages as containers for »objectively« existing contents, then they are »objective« for all – for the person who deposits them, and the one who retrieves them. If the other does not »understand properly«, the understandable tendency is to discredit that person as incompetent or a trouble-maker. »You don't understand me!« – Whoever talks like this controls what the success of communication is. This means that the relationship of the partners is asymmetrical. »Understanding« is decided by the speaker and not together with the listener. The goals of the speaker rule. At best people blame a »technical communication fault«. »He cannot listen properly.« they say. Here too, the speaker decides what is »right«. In the worst case it is annoying. The aggression level rises. The linguistic metaphor contained in »understand« turns out to be what it always was: the insistence of a monopoly right of interpretation. This one-sidedness is the claimed prerogative to reject what others get out of the message; the arrogance of someone who is right; the authority to decide what is be considered as the *true* interpretation and the *correct* perspective.

It is therefore a lot more useful to approach misunderstandings as an indication of the fact that we have failed continually to coordinate our inward maps, our personal experience. That shows how important feedback is.

»We understand each other« is an attractive illusion; in daily business it is dangerous. For normal work processes the illusion may suffice in order to cooperate relatively well. The difficulties arise in situations which are socially complicated, when there are disputes, difficult decisions, jittery markets, performance reviews, goal agreements. This illusion of understanding gives a false sense of security which can have deeply disturbing consequences. It opens the door to many disappointments and irritations. Especially in precarious situations, as when there are conflicts, the factor representing our subjectivity rules. Then in disastrous, mutual claims to the truth, mutual recrimination and self-justification which destroy integrity, the cat comes screaming out of the bag: »That is completely wrong!« But nobody can see wrongly. They just see differently. Starting from the concept »Understanding« means: being ready for a tough life full of disappointments.

Why do I write that? The company is »built« around understanding. Precisely in this internal corporate communication drama – in the belief: »The other must see it exactly the same way«, in the illusion: »Everyone is talking about the same thing«, in what is done: monologue, instructions, top-down information. The result: non-comprehension, incomprehension, disagreement, no commitment.

For our life in business there is another feature with many consequences: The essence of understanding is only secondly a linguistic phenomenon; primarily it reflects social emotions. Without a minimum of *wanted* community, without the *wish* to understand, without the inner readiness to bring together different ideas, not even a little understanding is probable. But for this we must first recognize the variability of individual constructs of reality.

Understanding is thus dependent on the quality of the *relationship*. Where sympathy is lacking and people are not taken seriously, where aversion predominates and people are treated like objects, barely anyone will be inclined to generate the recommended information supply in themselves, to let it approach them at all. Re-thinking. The emotional blockade refuses to accept the message. Max Frisch wrote, »Without goodwill, understanding is impossible.«

I cannot say it clearly enough: *It is not a question of understanding others.* Taking people seriously does not imply empathizing, interpreting, analyzing. I respect other people in their incomprehensibility. I respect their selfhood and its limits which are firmly drawn between us and which link and separate us. Between partners the issues are: Where do you stand? Where do I stand? What are your interests? What are my interests? On which point do we cooperate? For this purpose I need not understand (in an analyzing or interpreting sense). For this purpose I must hear. For this purpose I must state.

»I understand« is therefore not a meaningful statement. The only meaningful statement the observer can make, if the other does what the observer wants him to do, is: »You understand.« Strictly speaking, only then can one know, what one has said, when one hears the other's words or sees what they do. This recognition was expressed by Norbert Wiener very aptly: »How am I supposed to know what I said without having heard the answer to it?« Understanding means responding.

How important it is that within a team certain values, patterns and rules, briefly, a certain »reality« is shared, is obvious. Choose a reality which everyone gladly shares in! You must re-invent and justify this reality over and over again. This model is the »basis of the business.« You must be able to depend on the fact that the other is talking »approximately« about the same thing which you are talking about. But if, in your daily life, you are aware of the fact that you cannot expect people to share a common perspective you will be all the more careful in your approach. *You will build a common reality carefully, exercising mutual respect.* Making any potential gaps in understanding as small as possible by avoiding anything which makes understanding even more difficult than it already is. For this purpose the inner assumption that »understanding is improbable« and the resulting curiosity for the other perspective. You must *want* to oppose incomprehension.

Communication

The assumption, however, that all recognition has constructive features does not provide any basis at all for the much stronger claim that recognition is *nothing other* than free invention. I am not an enthusiastic defense attorney for the arbitrary play of interpretative nonsense. It would be itself despotic because of its arbitrariness: the democracy of semantic twisting. Describing a situation responsibly (»responding«), with good will towards the other, in other words replying in a responsible manner, does not at all mean relating to reality in terms of shadow boxing or jugglery. It means putting effort into maintaining relationships, removing obstacles and functional support.

From the fact that reality cannot be read independently of the observer, somewhere »out there«, it does not follow by any means that all reality is basically an illusion, fiction or purely a matter of taste. The only consequence is that reality is generated by communication and its usefulness tested. The cyberneticist Ernst von Glasersfeld distinguishes in an enlightening manner between »to be right« and »to fit«: »A key ›fits‹ if it opens the lock. Fit describes the ability of the key, but not that of the lock. From professional burglars we know all too well that there are a lot of keys which are shaped differently than ours but nonetheless can open our doors.« So we do not »unlock« any messages. We search, or more accurately, we *form* at best, keys which fit. So, at issue here is the question of usefulness, not of reality. »Fits all right«, is a Frankish expression.

Correspondingly, the »key to others« is promised by many management consultants who say, with the complicity of psychologists, »want to understand«, meaning »want to control«. This sort of consciousness does not want to talk *to* employees but rather *convince* them. There you can find such sentences as: »Treat your employees as you would like to be treated yourself.« This opinion is spread everywhere, it can be read in management handbooks all over. Everyone nods thoughtfully and considers this proverb to be the core revelation of western leadership wisdom. But at best it is dumb. Blindly arrogant, they make their own experiences binding for everyone else. Personal values are raised to the level of universally valid premises. With what right? Because someone is the boss? Because some people have always believed that they were a little more right? That is just simple, and no longer effective.

But is the alternative valid? For example: Treat your employees the way *they* would like to be treated? That would also be ineffective. It would also just be a half-measure. It is more practical to turn your attention to the employees. You could ask them. To do this you really have to be interested in what their perspectives are (lat. »inter-esse« means »to be between«). To do this you must – a linguistic sensation – become »acquainted« with them. Their experiences, expectations and interests are basically no less important for the cooperative effort than yours. You can agree together on rules. Namely because it is impossible for us to make objective statements about reality, we must continuously and communicatively negotiate »realistic« reality models with our cooperation partners. For reality is that which is effective, and this effectiveness is generated by communication. Established together as useful. Reality is thus the results of agreement.

Each person understands what they understand, exclusively on the basis of their inward map. Communication is therefore comparable with coordinating inner maps. Talking with each other means: mutually adjusting inner maps. Always aware of the fact that there is an incomprehensible remainder with which we must live. To make this as small as possible is the art of dialogue.

Dialogue

»Knowledge of blindness is a prerequisite,« said Heinz von Foerster, »for vision.« If you are interested in successful communication it is substantially more practical (as I hope I have shown) to assume the existence of basic incomprehension. The more you tend to agree that understanding is improbable, the more you will – paradoxically – make an all out effort to understand. The more you will really listen to the other person. The more you will repeatedly check that you both – more or less – mean the same thing. You will do everything to *facilitate* understanding, and avoid everything which makes understanding less probable than it is anyway.

Justitia's reputation also rose after her blindness.

If you assume that there are objective truths, that there is something called understanding, then a monologue is sufficient, informing, no-deposit-no-return communication. Strictly speaking you do not need the partner, for you have, dependent on your abilities, »the whole truth« at your disposal. The other person's contribution is not very valuable anyway. The main source for the communication chaos in many fields of business: »I am stating the truth, and you have your opinion.« One person thinks he clearly sees the truth. But he is just inventing it. Even in problem solving the unspoken pattern is present: someone has the right solution. Question: Who? »My solution is the right one, but the others have not realised it yet.« Such an attitude presumes *one sole correct answer* which exists somewhere »out there«. But there is nothing »out there«.

How can communication succeed? Not by any techniques. Only by respecting the other person's individuality. The fact of incomprehension formally compels dialogue. If both know that, it can work. It is like performances of the same ballet, the same symphony or the same string quartet: not until you have included different perspectives, different interpretations and compared them with each other do you enter the realm of enlightenment.

Monologing shrinks your world. Dialoging enlarges it. All this points to a managerial style based on dialogue. That is not a socially romantic wish to re-design the corporation, building on a morally sound humanization of the work place. The situation simply requires it. The re-introduction of responsibility into business compels a radical change from hierarchical *instructions* to understanding in dialogue about *tasks*. In everyday work this means: lively debates, similar to conflicts, frequently take the place of unilateral communication. Similar to conflicts? Instead of »discussions« in which winners and losers are always produced and in which exclusive claims to truth compete, we need »dialogues«: thinking together, finding new perspectives together. Everyone is right – that does not mean indifference and lack of interest. The exact opposite: it means feeling such an intense interest in the others that I no longer compel them to accept my value judgements. Not on moral grounds, but because it is simply practical. Instead of saying: »What makes you say that?«, saying, »Interesting, I have not examined the matter from this point of view yet!«

Information – communication

The talk about »information« presumes you could create an idea in your head, put it into words, transport it to your interlocutor by sound waves, who hears the words, decodes them and then stores them 1:1 in the brain. The old transmitter-receiver model of communication psychology was constructed on the basis of this understanding. People may have wondered repeatedly why that did not work so well, but largely they were satisfied with the explanation that the other probably had not listened so well, or the speaker had not found the right words. Wrong! The recipient of the message completely re-designs the message. They write the words heard across their own mental transparency and thus »invent« an independent message. They add meaning to it, interpret the message. Looked at clearly this means:

There is no such thing as information.

I do not write this to broaden linguistic conventions but to expand the understanding of the world which lies behind them. In fact, no information or messages are »carried« as if from one container to another. They are only impulses and there is no saying how individuals will perceive them or react to them. A word is a magician's hat, into which someone puts a rabbit and someone else pulls out a dove.

So there is nothing but *communication*. Each receiver is simultaneously a transmitter. Each receiver, a creator. The inward defines the outward. Each reader is reading, here and now, another book. A book which contains no information, merely impulses for one's own creativity ... and in a manner which I may not always like. It was fascinating for me to see the extent of the discrepancies between what different people interpreted from reading »The Myth of Motivation«, including thoughts I had not intended to convey at all. Some of these annoyed me considerably. Not infrequently, my impression was, that some of them had read another book altogether. Thus, many readers will also find here just what they, in fact, had always known.

Just as striking: to experience that participants from seminars remember metaphors as especially important which I had only mentioned in an aside and which, from my perspective, were only of secondary importance. But I recognized a fact: during seminars everyone watches their own inner home movie.

The subjectively linked nature of all wisdom, truths and values has important consequences. Let us take as an example the buzzword in corporate culture discussions, »vision«.

Prior to vision

The company needs new values! Anyone who wants to lead in business today must have »visions« and use them to resist the decay of the traditional work ethic. The suspicion that the internal composition of the company could have something to do with irresponsible leadership disappears behind the stage setting of corporate identity, and a chorus of shadowy wailing women appears on the stage. Their refrain: The world has become so complicated.

To improve the mood one apparently has to lower demands. This is how the corporate culture carnival tours up and down the country, all year long, wearing its favorite mask, »vision«. If at an earlier time someone had said that they had a vision, they would have been sent to a doctor. Today they are sent to a doctor if they have *no* vision. Then they are considered a »non-visionary leaders«. The evasive adjective »visionary« ennobles even the most simple-minded drivel about the future, transforming it into a message of salvation. Interchangeable. Flat. Without obligation. The actual contents of these visions are known primarily by the noise they make.

To what end? The function is clear: reducing corporate complexity, channeling the independent dynamic of drifting corporate units, a need for identity, compensation for fading intimacy, conveying of a sense of security in the feeling of belonging, vitalizing the whole system. Although the two Harvard professors, John P. Kotter and James L. Heskett, fail to find any positive correlation between corporate vision and corporate success, no matter: the future party is in full swing.

The corporate managers may rarely be able to resist the temptation to define suitable contents as standards, top-down. More importantly: It often happens that they pound them into their employee's minds as if trying to re-enact the giving of the ten commandments to Moses. Any cheering is subdued. The vision becomes »a matter of belief«. Management must then »persuade«

everyone, overcoming any resistance and skepticism. The escape into authoritatively established »values«, which, in fact, are not jointly agreed upon guidelines but orders, originating somewhere, usually at the top level, testifies to little more than the thick authoritarian atmosphere of mental back rooms. When I read words which are loaded with historical meaning such as »re-education« to the idea of community or the »anchoring« of values I still get a shock.

Am I oversensitive? That may be. Yet it is sometimes urgently necessary to be somewhat oversensitive. People who seem to perspire this sort of escapism should try talking with residents of the former East Germany, who were sold real compulsory conformism for decades as visions. (»Formerly it was called *»plan supplement«*, today the English term, *»revised budget«* is used.) But apparently, in Germany of all places, decades of available experience that any framework of ideas imposed from above breaks up on the real experience of a different individual reality are insufficient to discredit the modern go-getter dream of a designed company: extensive quality here and now, market leadership one year later, and, en passant, radical change in company culture.

The vision idea is based on the belief that employees identify with the corporate goals. This conviction, in turn, is based on the belief in a unitary view of the organization. For this reason, the currently fashionable pastoral letter mentality emphasizes common values, rituals, symbols and mythologies which are intended to act like adhesive to bond together all the corporate members marching in the same direction: revealed clarity of purpose.

The subject-dependency of all wisdom, however, determines, before anything else, the individual as the location at which reality and purpose are produced. All sense of purpose is created by the individual and tied to subjectivity. It is always »I« who attributes meaning to the world. In this context people speak of »attributing« meaning and not of »accepting« meaning.

But, in the executive suites, adventurist generalizations are articulated which oppose the corporate collective to the concrete, detailed work of day-to-day business. If we look at any corporate culture mission statements it is not foreseeable, judging from the argument up to this point, how any one reader will react, since these texts do not »penetrate their consciousness«, but merely give people pause for their own thought. This explains the ineffectiveness of many »messages« which come down on employees like avalanches, triggered quarterly by CEOs.

As a practical example I quote a sentence which can be found worded more or less the same way in many company booklets: »Employees are the most important resource in our company.« (Nobody laughs.) There is no danger that this sentence will not get a round of applause from everyone. But what does it mean? Does it say anything? Does it contain any information? And if it says something – does it make the meaning of this statement at least somewhat clear? I invited one company's employees to put on paper their reactions to this sentence, in short, telegraphic comments. A few excerpts:

»Terrific! Too beautiful to be true.«
»Platitude from the CEO, completely lacking in credibility.«
»The sentence is right, but at our company employees are not treated accordingly.«
»Blah blah. Employees are just a means to an end.«
»This is an insult. People are the company, and not some sort of input givers.«
»Right. Resources are there to be consumed.«
»This is not the case yet, but we are on the right path.«
»Better than employees = factor of production.«

In a group of employees made up of 14 people no two reactions were in any way similar to each other, either in their substance or their wording! The subjective link of our response – our individual respons-ibility – uncovers the visionary firmament of the company as adolescent absurdity. People are not trivial machines. Meaning cannot – as we have seen – be »commanded«, but must be *created* by every employee on a strictly individual basis. There are no common values laid out for all time. There are only *discussions about values*, i. e. we must the keep the discussion about values alive and constantly bring up relevant issues.

Where all kinds of nonsense are loudly and ambitiously spread about »meaning« (»Communication in the decade of meaning«!), it has always been doubtful whether the general vision song and dance about building up and boosting business had anything sensible as its object. But the hidden price is high. As a reminder: on the basis of a market economy the purpose of companies is to produce goods and services and sell them. What applies here is the economic principle. That is the basis of business. That must be clear between the partners in the company. The individual can then add a personal sense of purpose to this overall purpose. This is optional. But there is no overall corporate measure for the production of purpose in the company necessary. It is even damaging, *because it clouds both transparency and personal responsibility.*

What is important for the issue of individual responsibility in the company, is that the vision or the corporate identity are part of the long tradition of finding purpose in external forces, comparable with revelations from God. The goal is for all employees to be emotionally synchronized, moving shoulder to shoulder behind the corporate vision, which is a defense against anything different, finally an extermination of individuality following the Japanese example. Personal responsibility, on the other hand, results from *one's own* decision, *one's own* response, not calling upon a higher authority. That is the difference. Quasi-religious redemptions relieve us also from our personal responsibility. Commitment, farewell!

Identification?

For a non-perspective corporate culture which believes it can build on clarity, »conveying« a sense of purpose and »transparent relations«, self-conscious and autonomous personalities are the fungus of anarchy. They therefore prefer static, hierarchical forms of domination. The subordinates »subordinate themselves« to the superiors. They are supposed to »become one« with the whole. That was primarily the ideology of communism, that system of exploitation sanctified by social resentment. Its central idea is »identification«.

But the return to a kind of de-personalized »oneness« and the promotion of pre-rational ideas of community undermines any form of commitment. To say it clearly:

Commitment is not identification.

People who identify with something, in the manner which is required by the spreading culture of employee confusion, are »beside themselves«. Identification implies a substantial degree of self-denial. In a symbiotic melting pot the limit between individuals become vague for the sake of the »larger« unit. »I sacrifice myself for the company« is the bottom line. Correspondingly logical is the employee consciousness of themselves as victims.

They are then ready for the many disappointments – at each and every moment when the idealized overall picture of »their« company does not correspond to raised expectations. That was possible to observe very well at Bosch or Henkel, for example, whose patriarchal corporate cultures and the lay-offs begun in 1992 led to apocalyptic irritations among employees: »A world collapses.« It is also known from organization psychology that the demand to identify with tasks, products or even with whole companies erodes people's sense of identity and sense of purpose, if the products are taken off the market or teams are broken up.

A corporate culture based on individual perspectives – as suggested here – recognizes each individual employee as an in dividual, distinct from the company. The vocabulary of such a corporate culture includes such terms as creativity, flexibility, organism, dynamics. Its core idea is *relationship*. It acts as an interface between the pressures of a de-personalizing greater whole and the indecisiveness of the detached observer. People who enter a relationship decide *in favor of something*, assume responsibility, take part. But they take »their part«, i. e. they acknowledge clear, recognized individual limits, which at the same time mark the boundaries of negotiations.

The ability to withdraw improves negotiating skill. An overall view and decisiveness is not possible without it. Its basis is conscious freedom of choice. But also choice of where one belongs: included, therefore, is also a bit of fear of loss and exclusion (many MBA job hoppers lack it). The we-feeling is created from the decided agreement on a common game and the agreed rules of the game. So it is a kind of intra-corporate *constitutional patriotism*. A mature, conscious decision in favor of one company: There we are negotiating partners. There we are respected and taken seriously. The rules create a balance between give and take.

Only in a relationship can duty become commitment. Only in a relationship can accountability become individual responsibility. Only in a relationship is durable, long-term and conscious commitment possible. So if your issue is commitment and individual responsibility: they only exist in a corporate culture based on individual perspective.

The Pragmatic Section

At the marketing conference of a major beverage distributor there are conference refreshment coolers on the table, as usual. Soon those present noticed that there are no openers. The managing director reproaches the marketing director, it was his responsibility to see to it that his employees had seen to it ...

Agreed, the employees are themselves responsible. But is not their supervisor also responsible? The position of this book is: yes, but not for placing openers in the coolers or for giving detailed instructions to employees, but for creating an environment which helps the employees to commit themselves, to act on their own initiative, to demonstrate commitment in their work.

For commitment requires social prerequisites. It is easier if the individual is not left standing all alone, if he knows he has the support of several others – no matter how few. Just as a corporate culture based on commitment is not possible without the involvement of many individuals, the individual also needs encouragement: an environment which makes success and solidarity probable.

Managers, because of their position in the hierarchy, are primarily responsible for creating these pre-requisites. The conditions of possibility for commitment. *Conditions of possibility* – that is not a show of modesty, but an insight that individual responsibility can neither be pulled down off the shelf or »made« in any other way. Finally, it always remains a matter of individual initiative and responsible action.

If you are a manager, ask yourself: do you promote enterprise, civic courage? Or do you prefer to float aimlessly in the stagnant waters of conformism?

Farewell to the bellwether

> *Whoever walks in another persons footsteps,*
> *leaves no impression.*

This is the recommendation: entrepreneurs to the front! We need entrepreneurs! Role models! Henkel! Grundig! Neckermann! Nixdorf! The companies articulate a need for tradition. They are cleaning out their mental-historical attics in their search for pioneer ancestors, founders, pioneer thinkers and doers who convey a sense of tradition and solidity. The alarmist crisis talk swears again by Schumpeter's »creative destroyer«. The *manager magazin* has opened, page by page – copying the American magazine *Fortune* – a »Business Hall of Fame«. All over, the renaissance of the »great man« can be felt, the reincarnation of the neoconservative metaphor of »either-you-got-it-or-you-ain't«. Employee orientation? That's history. Today what you need is: charisma, personality, charm. The return to *role models*, the simplifying urge to personify: if there is any common denominator in the business press then it must be the appeal to the role model function of managers, who in particular are supposed to bridge the gap between the model of desired forms of behavior and the really existing social disaster. Managers as role models: there is barely a more suitable object with which to illustrate the paradigm change in a company which is structured around the principle of individual responsibility.

Masculine muscle

Looked at historically the role model postulate has its origin in a time of clearly hierarchical allocation and subordination, when people still said »subordinate« (and meant it), typical for patriarchal structures, basic military formations (Shut your eyes and keep running! Go for it!). It has the same direction as the desire for hierarchy, authority and elitist thinking. For the role model grows analogously to its ability to intimidate. So it is no doubt a relic from the corporate culture of iron secondary virtues which were obligatory for the generation born previous to 1945.

As a consequence, »to be a role model« is an explicitly masculine associated figure of speech (just as illusions of grandeur occur much more rarely in women than in men). In a way the role model idea, then, appears to be the opposite of the individual and spontaneous, which embodies what Greek mythology imagined to be the female power of creation. For the role model is not the individual but the simplifying generalization. The personification of a principle. Despite understandable objections from women, for the present it can be said that this exemplary person is a man.

Management principles: exemplary

Yes, they should be »role models« again, our managers, more than ever. Models of virtue, morality and values. Günter Mordhorst, Chairman of the Board of Directors at Varta AG, a typical example: »Authority should … be deduced from the personal example of the leader.« If you do not have these personal giants on hand, they are artificially created: management principles as highly polished substitute role models. The embarrassingly obscene »employee of the month« – borrowed from the socialist Stakhanovite girls and »Heros of Socialist Labour«. The canon, approved as a prototype, usually reflects the career experiences of top management (so it is a reflection of the past) or is poured out as platitudes originating from so-called healthy common sense. I do not know a single booklet of these heavily moralistic role model substitutes which does not tell managers what their overall activity is – yes, right: to be a role model.

Well, turning to role models has always been a sign of insecurity. Slumps and recessions, in particular, tend to trigger an intense demand for men with a follow-me aura who alone can see the big picture or who claim to. They are supposed to balance the insecurity of the group as a super-ego with suggestive power (sigh, ours are such mental midgets!), and radiate security and trustworthiness. People want to work fast; they want to get ahead; they do not want to waste any time.

Why are people making this backwards somersault in organizational psychology now, of all times? The new lack of the big picture, the new randomness undermines people's orientation. Many companies are reacting to the erosion of general social values and current economic downturns with an old-new elite orientation with which they pile up reverse stabilizing value pyramids. The current high demand for polite behavior and proper etiquette training sessions to lend post-modern managers a wrinkle-free market appearance is no accident. This is evidence of the crisis.

But not only this: when, in leadership seminars, I ask the participants, what in their view, is the most important attribute for leadership, the majority answer: »Being a role model!« Furthermore, at a large Savingsbank whose 150 managers indicated which characteristics they considered to be absolutely necessary for a manager, opinions were clear: managers had to be role models, foremost as *specialists*, then, next in importance, but hardly less important, as *people*. (Often I have the impression they only mean »work longer«. When you become a manager you apparently show your willingness to suffer.)

The strain of vanities

Expert role model? Whoever has chosen the expert role model to be his professional ideal has, today, a rocky road through life indeed. The half-life of expertise is shortening dramatically in all fields. We assume today that human knowledge doubles roughly every 4.5 years. More than 90 percent of scientists, who have ever lived on this earth, are still alive today. Anyone who, under these conditions, wants to be a role model of expertise in his field will get back pains from the constant pressure he has to bear. Winning this competition is impossible. You cannot conduct an orchestra and, simultaneously play the first violin (unless your name is Johann Strauß; but that was yesterday).

Of course, managers still must know what game is being played in their line of business. Certainly they should also add to their expertise by attending seminars and courses. But »role model«? Why do they have employees in the first place? Oh yes, they are short of time; they would really like to do everything themselves. Anyway, the maximum of excellence is defined by themselves. This must lead to freezing up. The burn-out is waiting. Poor boss! But as we already know: the genuine hero belongs to the realm of tragedy. Only a handful of those raised to the level of role model could ever enjoy their fame during their own lifetimes. These managers are the crown of creation.

Know-it-alls

One could say that this is the individual's problem. But for the company the situation becomes precarious when the still highly dynamic Peter principle makes the expert screwdriver operator into a supervisor of screwdriver operators. The company then usually has two problems: one less good screwdriver operator and one more poor manager. The manager then forces the »one best way of driving screws«, his own of course, the good example, onto the employees, not merely as a good example but as a rule: »You see, this is how I've been so successful!« Such a boss is a steady source of demotivation for his employees. As the manager in charge of screwdriver operations and know-it-all he flattens everyone else who wants to do it differently, in their own way. This is especially problematic if one imagines what kind of supervisors the younger employees, after a comparatively better and more highly individualized educational background, will come up against.

In addition and most importantly: the search lights of the »learning company« cast doubt on the role model prose of German management cultures. For role models not only want to *be* role models – they also want to *remain* role models. Role models make sure that the others are always catching up. They do everything to keep a respectful distance between them and their employees – in terms of expertise as well. Their continuing education activism *has* a purpose: to keep the employees at a distance. These bosses will do anything to *prevent* their employees from developing.

To give a concrete example: in a role model culture the employee improvement idea comes very close to lese-majesty. The employee suggestion committee (a weed which took root in the organizational psychology of the early industrial period) will, finally, always fail because of this contradiction. Self-staged professional arrogance carefully watches over its expertise.

Personnel freezer

The head chef among the managers (»Here the head chef does the cooking himself!«) frequently enough justifies his existence on the basis of the weakness of his employees. He thus has absolutely no interest in employee development. He will place himself in the center of all the energy lines, following ancient field commander ideology, and will develop the employee potential of group either not at all or only insufficiently. Thus the demand for role models as a basis of leadership turns out to be the *negation of personnel development*, its fundamental contradiction. It means the same as the demand for its elimination.

Invest in employee skills? Delays are dangerous! Precisely because of the role model mentality of many supervisors there are widespread inhibitions against personnel development which is really intended to change things. How should partner networking and role models coexist? How can these match: employees loyal to the model and intrapreneuship? Clearly: the chatter about role models is one of the best camouflaged, most effective – since unrecognized – obstacles in the way of learning organizations. With such a waste of ability no company in future will have much chance of turning a profit.

What remains? Can managers at least provide role models as human beings? This is arrogance pure and simple. What right does anyone have to claim to be the role model for someone else? Because he is a manager? Looked at this way, the idea is simply absurd.

Self-renunciation

There are however quite a few managers who milk themselves to the point of self-renunciation in order to act as a role model. Yes, this is a literal form of »self« renunciation – they want to live up to the model. Over-work is the minimum stake. A role model shows no weaknesses. It is *always* a role model. Human emotions? Disappointment? Insecurity? Palaver! Instead: symbolic action played to the grandstands. A presentation culture of successful self-rigidifying in which nothing is done because it is considered appropriate and important but because it pleases the others, and thus can be considered exemplary. Being a role model means lying.

As the wise man said: *every investment in an image is an investment in your own prison cell.* The self-created role model is intended to decorate, provide a standard – but also has a standardizing effect on the person acting it – the investor. Acting as an example requires managers to engage in a high degree of self-denial in response to the continuous pressure to conform. It is exhausting to allow your professional life to be ruled by a style code. The drilled-in behavioral scripts often turn into the perversion of what one might call personal identity. So it is no wonder that these heroes are constantly running the danger of going off the deep end. Often the rising star pays the price of poor health, but more often of a loss of integrity. (Just imagine, you have to do things for years of which you are not convinced; on the other hand, completely suppress things which you feel comfortable with!) The presumed gain in prestige is purchased at the price of restrictions in his scope to act and, finally, with a loss of freedom.

People who wear themselves out for the crowd, by setting an example, and expect to shame others into action or to convert them into ambitious followers: are they suffering like martyrs? No, they are staging the suffering of a martyr, says Nietzsche, and thus the result is – something disingenuous. Where the impression of authenticity and purity is created, there is a hidden agenda, and the effects are calculated. Self-exhaustion meant to inspire others: this deal openly stinks and completely undermines any credibility.

Quite a number of managers have indeed introjected this role model expectation to such an extent that they themselves feel like walking amateur actors, reduced to what has been assigned to them from outside, prototypes of expectations, reduced to stereotypes, their humanity nearly extinguished – and, in their own way, dead. The return to role models is genuinely reminiscent of eulogies. How do they put it? »He will always be example for us.« That is the diction found in obituaries. In life, deceased, frozen into a character statuette, conveniently available on demand. Previously it was said: »For Germans in an age of despair« Today: »There is a desperate need (!) to reveal the real entrepreneurs.«

Or: »What we need are managers with visionary power who can convey to employees the meaning of their work.« Hurray! Follow him! Only the dead can serve as a slick role model without tarnishing the image by behaving all too humanly. Highly charged dynamism makes any cracks visible. But that is how the gravestone glows. (Well, people who die earlier are dead longer.)

Whether martyrdom is somehow useful is doubtful; that it does damage, is certain. It is obvious that the suppression and self-castration which accompanies it is able to mobilize a considerable potential for aggression. The continuous pressure to conform causes people to become strangers to themselves, which can explain to a large extent the spread of communicative brutality in our companies. The result: the »After-us-the-deluge« mentality in many executive offices; and the wasteland is growing.

Managing as parenting

People who need a role model do not need to exert themselves to find out what they themselves really think. They do not need to compare, weigh advantages against disadvantages, justify the substance of their work, or its goals, or hold any convictions. They only need to parrot suggestions. That is simply logical. For role model thinking comes from the context of »upbringing«. A management handbook, impressively going into its third edition in 1994, contains the statement: »A good boss does not shout at his employees at every opportunity, but brings them up by setting a good example.« Apart from the fact that this sentence makes me nauseous: there it is, the upbringing context, in which immature kids ought to be »raised«, who look to values, which are defined for them by others, according to yardsticks, which others provide for them. It perpetuates the model learning of the parent-child relationship. Reducing people to infants as a principle of leadership. In this context it is only logical when one of the largest German chemicals companies rewards women employees for their suggestions by handing out pocket makeup mirrors.

Psychologically, the role model is directed by a benevolent parent towards the conformist child in us. (Privately one has so often become exactly what one least wanted to become: the mirror image of one's parents.) The principles of child rearing are tacitly transferred to managers – as many managers automatically draw analogies between both areas anyway. This is reflected in the culture of keeping employees immature in many companies: managing as parenting.

A corporate culture supported by role models (no matter what kind they are) divides the whole working population into two: those who are role models or who create them artificially, and the others who do not act so exemplary and who quite obviously need the role model (the latter group is the majority). In clear terms: there are many employees in our company who need to aspire to being like a role model. The talk about role models disqualifies a share of the employees (the largest!) as needing a role model. Does anyone not feel the arrogance which is contained in this difference? Does anyone not sense the declaration of incapacity contained in the intention of being able to set before us a role model which we all should chase?

But the effect on productivity and motivation has an ironic twist: for the greatness of the one only consists in the fact that the other offers its smallness as a gift. The exemplary nature of the one is not sufficient; the other must – so that the role model becomes visible as such – present its defective nature, so to speak, at its feet. *Just as some only appear big because the others are stooping.* Once again, the results are passivity and lack of commitment. A classic example of incomplete thinking, installing simple solutions for complex phenomena, whose incidental consequences cancel out the desired effects. Or, in Peter Sloterdijk's words: »Because *we cause* such an enormous number of things to occur as we think, *we experience* the overall outcome as explosively unexpected.«

Many people are characterized by nothing if not an early Christian resistance to any challenges raised by individual responsibility. This includes a tendency to identify symbiotically with the role model; a yearning for security. Similar to that of a child. Many employees, who are adults in terms of calendar years, never mature beyond the stage of conventional imitation; they remain trainees forever, sometimes willing, and sometimes unwilling recipients of orders. Not only that, managers who just wanted to be a role model, then turn around and complain about their employees' lack of independence.

For every organization gains in freedom what the individual loses to it – but, at the same time, assuming the corresponding responsibility. The conscience is thus more or less subtly marked by company authority figures or sworn to adhere to authoritarian rules. The point is to »follow the leader«. That is the way they remain: behind. Always in second place. Adults are frozen in an adolescent condition, which cuts off possibilities and leaves employee potential unused. The role model control reduces adults to company marionettes which are open to any influence but which never take responsibility. Thus, the corporate culture oriented towards role models can be seen as a culture without commitment. The emphasis on managers as role models is the mark of Cain of immature organizations.

A variation on a well-known Brecht quotation: happy the company which needs no heroes.

Living imitations

The consequences of the role model idea for companies are simply catastrophic. For this mental image is based on the categorical error that role models are useful for achieving corporate goals.

Let us ask ourselves: are these the employees which we need, the kind that always follow behind, who are the copies of role models? The original always produces counterfeits. Living imitations: »Be like me!« Employees who do not learn by their own experience, by encountering themselves, but are impressed by the radiance of the role model. They are not creative, but mimic. They do not think, but parrot. Do such employees make a difference? Do they input something of their own? It is easy to slip on a path which has been worn smooth.

Such employees have traded in their own internal value concept for dependence on something else. But people who are dependent on something else easily lose their balance. People dependent on good role models are also dependent on bad ones. A nightmare: what happens if the role model turns out to be a person made of flesh and blood, with defects, weaknesses, or even deep flaws in character? What happens if the mask falls? The image of charismatic management personalities is especially in danger of simply falling away (see Lee Iacocca). People who need a role model testify only to their own weak sense of identity. They suppress their own uniqueness, their individuality and their possibilities.

This has consequences: a negative role model in a position high up in a hierarchy is considered frequently for a variety of reasons as »untouchable«. This immunity is well meant in short-term company interest, but it often leaves its mark on young

entrants to the company over generations who see in this negative role model what sort of characteristics apparently are rewarded in this company. Many companies are completely blind to these incidental and delayed consequences of their short-sightedness which result in a worthless model unintentionally having a substantial impact.

Another example may be the orientation towards the Japanese role model, which sails under the colors of lean management. With the enthusiasm for imitation of good Teutonic schoolkids the lean concepts of the Japanese are grafted onto a mature industrial culture where the social environment is completely incomparable with that of the »model«. One can only muster a weary smile in reaction to what is being tried out, the ahistorical stuff and the efforts to be »more Japanese than the Japanese.« Hardly a model for us: the long hours of workers in Japan, the extremely high work intensity, the »passing on« of the cost pressure to the suppliers, the social dumping, the company loyalty of the employees, the established seniority principle, patriarchal leadership forms, extreme pressure to conform and the absence of any autonomous interest group representation: none of this is either supported by a consensus in Germany, nor would it be capable of functioning – for good historical reasons, it seems to me. In our search for workable orientations Germany does not need to look to Japan: Prussian-German traditions are »closer« and have been available for some time. No, Germans must take their own path between Taylorism and Toyotism, a path informed and supported by their central European individualistic culture.

We're right behind you, Joe!

A corporate culture built on role models unintentionally creates dependence and employees who take too little responsibility and who have alienated their sense of personal identity. »Imitate!«

degrades the employees into dumb fools who apparently cannot be mobilized by any other means. Again: are those the kind of employees with which we want to face the future?

Doubtful effects: role model observers never take responsibility! They remain dependent on the directive issued by the idealized other. »I am doing this not because I consider it right but because he sets the example.« Or »I am not doing it, because the other is not doing it either.« Even for those who otherwise insistently cherish their own independence: »The directors should do it themselves first!« Especially in the case of negative models: the reference to the neighboring department which does not keep to the agreement either. Or: »If he does not follow the rules, then I don't have to either.«

Basically the core of the problem is: the demand for the role model is again an example of »Not-wanting-to-be-responsible.« »We're right behind you, Joe.« An example of the fact that not until the other has to change will I consider my own position at all. Individual responsibility? The poor model is all too frequently an argument used to remain passive. Role models necessarily produce lack of responsiveness and irresponsibility.

The extent of the contradictions in the on-going discussion can be seen quite clearly in the re-engineering concept put forward by Hammer/Champy who continuously want to move employees to take responsibility. The whole book is spiced with sentences like: »The leader promotes the re-engineering process with stirring speeches.« – »The top management must show the way by setting a good example.« – »Motivate people to take responsibility for the process and inspire your re-engineering team.« – »A leader must have a genuine leadership personality ..., who can inspire others to want what he wants to achieve.« – »Be daring, says the leader, and if anyone puts you under pressure, refer him to me.« A great show of responsibility.

The role model – A passive quality

Is that possible at all, what is being demanded everywhere, namely being a role model? Can anyone intentionally be a role model? That is extremely questionable, because it assumes that this model is perceived by all people more or less the same, as a »role model«. But the role model is never a fixed image which everyone sees in the same way. Everyone brings their own selves into the process of interpretation. Everyone creates another image of the other; and what one person considers a role model, the next person may not consider worthy of imitating at all; what appears a worthwhile goal to one, is worth nothing at all to another. Those who argue most fervently in favor of the role model quality of managers are frequently in the eyes of their employees everything but role models. Epistemologically the demand to be a role model is simply nonsense.

Nevertheless, would it be, quite apart from the problem of perception, possible? Of course not. To be a role model is not an active category, but a passive one. People are, at best, *made into* role models. If you are a manager, you will, under certain circumstances, not be able to prevent others from making you into their role model, that others see in you something exemplary for themselves – as an external allocation, attribution; but not as self-presentation. You do not make yourself into a role model, you are made into one by others. Being a role model is, at best, a passive quality, not an active one.

A leading model to follow behind can thus not be »set at the head« of a group (in either sense). If there is a role model, then individuals will choose it for themselves, according to individual criteria. Role models are not stars which create their own light, but, if at all, they are lanterns which we light within ourselves.

People who try to be active role models will, precisely by trying, fail. The (active) role model does not act, in order to act, but to be a role model; the point of emphasis is displaced, the motive for acting comes from outside; it wants to »appear« (a loaded word) to act; it stages its performance to have an affect on others. For this reason, it will fall short of having any effect. Employees in general are acutely sensitive to credibility. First and foremost to its absence.

Nevertheless, do we not need this canon of the exemplary? I am not ignoring the fact that in many companies exemplary behavior – often also referred to »presentability« – is considered a prerequisite for promotion and advancement. Of course I also know that many employees believe that they need role models (as a sort of substitute for father and mother). I am also aware of the fact that, in particular, poor examples set by supervisors, on the one hand, undermine the legitimacy of the leadership position, and, on the other, are frequently used to excuse any poor behavior on the part of the employees.

No matter – must we also promote this? Continue to require it in management guidelines which are raised to the level of a codex? Is it desirable that this ethical »should« be considered as an obligatory goal? Is this requirement still helpful and sensible in times of highly networked working structures, team organizations, international mobilization and increasing flexibility, flat hierarchies and larger gaps between levels of management, a value dynamic directed towards symmetry and partnership, considering the socialization processes which are meant to achieve early independence and clear-cut individualization? Furthermore can anyone seriously believe that those born between 1945 and 1965 who dominate management today, are a credible generation of role models? (Take a look how often the question on the subject of role models included in the popular personality questionnaires is left unanswered – for example in the Frankfurter Allgemeine Zeitung.) Basically skeptical of any morally worded ideals, stripped of ideology, pragmatic, raised in an ethics of all-encompassing selfhood, they are the dispassionately enlightened, with a generally ironic view of moral athletes. For them, there are no authoritative truths any more, merely subjective statements, attitudes, preferences. For them the traditional, value-creating role models were relieved of their duties ages ago. We don't need another hero.

Everyone knows the first reaction when someone is placed before them as a role model; openly or quietly they are trivialized, small defects are sought – to balance the situation of social inequality. It is not a question of being a role model. It is a question of being credible and genuine. It makes a difference whether you are genuine because you yourself think this is important – or whether you want to manipulate others. Credible managers promote the role model *in each individual.* Each employee is a unique personality. All employees may demand to have their uniqueness respected. An absolutely necessary prerequisite for genuine commitment is to break away from the continuous external leadership through role models and to take the responsibility for acting oneself. Thomas Banyacya, a Hopi elder, says: »No one can predict to what height you can soar, until you have spread your wings.«

And Emerson writes in his »Self-Reliance«: *»In every individual's education there comes the moment in which he becomes convinced that envy is ignorance, that imitation is suicide, that he must accept himself as his fate in joy and suffering; that, although the universe is full of good things, not a single nutritional grain can come to him without his effort, which he applies to the bit of earth which has been granted him to work. The power within himself is a new kind, and only he knows what he can do, and even he does not know this until he has exercised it.«*

This quotation is worth reading a second time.

Leadership goal: individual responsibility

What remains? Following a role model and taking responsibility are opposing terms. Companies must decide whether they want to work with a horde of dependent followers with little responsibility or whether they want to support autonomy, individual responsibility and commitment. And the individual managers? A role model can defend itself. They do not have to be the Hero of Labour if they do not want to. They can also do something:

- Speak with your employees about the snags of role modeling.
- Stop trying to please the others no matter what the price; do not sell your birth right to self-determination for the red pottage of following.
- Be genuine; ask yourself: »Am I only acting like this because I want to impress somebody?«
- Allow yourself *not* to meet other people's expectations from time to time.
- Do something unexpected on occasion; something which does not at all comply with your image. You'll see: it is really liberating.

Many managers feel complimented by being raised onto the pedestal of the role model. Responsible managers will make a point of preventing this kind of idealization, or at least keeping it to a minimum. They will do everything to keep the employees independent of themselves, and thereby more responsible. They will, instead of surrounding themselves with an aura of the perfect role model, remind their employees of the explorative and fragile, the personal dimension to their work. I am conscious of the irony when I remember how my first boss – my role model – one said: »I don't feel like playing the role model for you.«

Demands to bring down barriers can be heard everywhere: internationally, between countries, and within companies, through innovation and creativity. Why not in personnel policy as well? On this level, breaking down barriers means going beyond the role model – achieving adulthood. In companies, we also need individual identity formation in companies as a continuous learning process. I have no shadow of a doubt that we must change our frame of reference: rejecting the role model and turning to an understanding of management whose central idea is *individual responsibility*.

To honor someone you must go beyond them.

Addendum I

Some people might well sophistically turn my argument against me by saying a manager who does not want to be a role model could, by adhering to these ideas, become a role model under another heading. My answer to this is: problems cannot be solved by the same sort of thinking which caused them in the first place. Twisting things like this is only another form of dependency whose contents have been modified and where individual responsibility is still quietly avoided. But (and it is not difficult for me to admit this): no boss is so bad that he could not serve as a negative example.

Addendum II

Popular at the moment is the »bogeyman«, the negative version, so to speak, of the role model. Since there is a chronic short supply of consensus in companies, in many place – greetings from Kienbaum – bogeymen must fill in as a substitute basis for reaching a consensus. Anyone who listens is told the old story of the use of a flail, which you should beat especially in hard times, to generate harmony within the company. That has the function of pretending to the employees that they are consummating an act of patriotism when they vigorously load the canon to fire off a volley at the enemy company.

This follows the old »tattle-tale principle«: *the other kid did it!* All violence comes from the enemy. He threatens us, not the other way round. Of course, both sides think this. At the same time, no mention is made of the fact that the image of the bogeyman is our own creation. Again we can wash our hands in innocence: we are not responsible for this situation! Under the pressure of circumstances, enemy aggression, and shorter and shorter deadlines, everything which might help to stave off the threat becomes urgently urgent. A consensus of defense is achieved. This empowers a few – »those in responsibility« – to think some order or another is »necessary«, which, then, the many others should execute. Bogeymen are a genuine gold mine of necessities. No time for long empty talk! It is well-known that the authority of a government over its citizens is based largely in its power to wage war.

I would rather not write here about the unspeakable appeal to the most primitive instincts, about the poverty of the arguments, about the historical parallels (we had this already: July, 1914). But it is simply unintelligent to proceed like this: what happens when the enemy turns out to be far less wicked than you require him to be. If you set up a bogeyman you are making the company massively dependent on pressure from outside. Here, too: you do not build on inner strength, but on the attitude necessitated by an outside force, in this case a defensive stance.

In addition, it is a mistake to believe that the aggressive energy only impacts on the competitor. A bogeyman atmosphere also incites aggression within the company. Under the weight of the overstock of psychological aggression one's own company suffers most. The bogeyman is a spiritual assistant for self-deception.

Supervisors, managers

The »supervisor« model is the initiation into stupidity as a condition of normalcy.

In the manager rosary of canonized buzz words the terms »supervisor« and »manager« are usually used as synonyms. Behind them, however, are very specific and, I think, distinctively different models. Below I develop both concepts as contrary ideal types because I am mainly interested in a few essential differences; in practice, a wide range of mixed forms are the rule.

No longer in production

A supervisor is firstly nothing more than the result of the organizational structure, whereby the hierarchical disciplinary dimension is emphasized. His authority is defined by the position. This, in turn, is linked to an office which receives as »potestas« from above. This places him in a »superior« position to the employees.

The concept »supervisor« is a figure of speech meaning »over« – and, in the same sense, »better«. The motto is: »I am better than the others!« The hierarchically superior does not necessarily have the authority of someone who is actually »better«, but stands on the claim to authority from the fact that the hierarchy expects him to be better. Supervisors, therefore, frequently exploit the observed or merely alleged weakness of their employees, even sometimes – nasty accusation, this – consciously showing them off, at least to *appear* »better«. This is logical: they justify their own existence by the inadequate performance of their employees. Many supervisors are serial killers of human intelligence. The employees grow increasingly demoralized, increasingly defeated and have less and less enthusiasm at these tediously bland events.

In the »supervisor« model the subject is isolated and alone in the environment. Employees are the objects in this environment. They are hardly perceived themselves as agents, but rather as »factors« (Martin Heidegger), with which the agent works. They are »personnel«. That is »treated« in the same way you handle a computer: with the help of command menus. To this end the supervisors check the user handbook from time to time. Or they peek into psychology. This gives them helpful tips how to manage and operate the objects until they do what the supervisor thinks is right. Supervisors talk *about* people whose awareness is different. They don't talk *with* them. They have something to say, but little to convey.

This awareness shapes their relations with their environment by means of language: there is a »subordinate« (who is only supposed to give, but usually does not provide the right thing); the »direct reports«, they »report to me«, »they work for me«, »I have them under me«. American managers even refer to »hands«.

The supervisor culture is distinguished by its orientation towards the facts and the tasks at hand; it is primarily based on expertise. A promotion to supervisor is thus construed as a reward for performance. But performance is, so to speak, a moment immobilized in the past; it says very little about future performance under modified (leadership) working conditions. (Unfortunately companies still promote more based on performance rather than potential.)

A change of models

A supervisor is legalized by the hierarchy. He receives this legalization »from above«. Managers, on the other hand, *can*, but need not be the product of organizational structure. Their acceptance emerges from their personal qualities, not from their position. Their acceptance is not necessarily related to their official title but is due to their competence, which employees recognize, an »auctoritas«. They are therefore not necessarily legalized by the hierarchy, but *legitimized*. This legitimization comes »from below«.

In this way the employees enter the discussion as a determining factor for successful management activity. Those who are led are the legitimizing authority. That is the essential difference in relation to the supervisor – in one sentence:

> *You do not have competence to lead,*
> *it is given to you.*

The sole authority on leadership which really counts is the one which is voluntarily and consciously granted by those being lead. A promotion to the rank of supervisor can, at best, give you the authority associated with the position, but never personal authority. But leadership competence is awarded to you by the employees. You are dependent on their »response«. The employees *choose* whether they grant you this right to lead them. If they remove this right you may still be their supervisor. But you are no longer their manager.

Yet much more important is: you can no longer do your job. You can no longer fulfill your task of cultivating the potential of your employees for the benefit of the company. Moderating, coordinating, linking up – you can do none of these things if your employees do not recognize your competence to lead. Then you find yourself absurdly suspended in mid-air.

In the general feasibility insanity this sort of supervisor is sent to leadership seminars to boost his leadership skills. So-called behavioral training sessions seem to be the proven means to this end. Usually a trainer is bought in, sets up a video camera, at the sight of which most seminar participants react in the same way an ordinary motorist reacts when he sees a police car in his rearview mirror. Then the training starts – comparable to football players practicing corner kicks. That works too, can be understood, is logical and promises additional competence: no doubt better than nothing, for there are individual prerequisites for successful leadership. But the effect is limited because: you do not have managerial competence ...

As a result there are far more supervisors than managers: not every supervisor is a manager. In the age of projects, teams, networks and flowing structures the prevalent idea will increasingly be: not every manager is simultaneously a supervisor ... all the way to groups released from the hierarchy in which a specialist can also be a team leader.

In the model »manager« the subject does not perceive other subjects as part of the furniture but as other people. The subject is aware of itself as linked into a network of relationships between partners who are existentially equal. This type of manager is not »better«, but simply does another job.

Having this other-people attitude, the subject understands the outward world/employees as his equal, towards whom he has a taking-part attitude. Then he encounters his partnert with respect and attention because he is on the same plane. Respect for others is the respect towards oneself. If he violates the dignity of the other person/co-worker he also simultaneously and necessarily violates his own dignity. The word »co-worker«, has, however, lost its original participatory meaning implying equality in rank. Today it designates inferiority, deprecation, a label for anyone who is not a manager, and is »only« there to co-work. With this other-people attitude described here the sense of partnership can be re-established: in the sense of »together« and »sharing«.

Please the customer

Ask yourself: who decides the quality of a product? The customer. Who decide the quality of a service? The customer. Who decides the quality of leadership? Don't hesitate: the customer. And the manager's customer is: the employee.

Does the employee buy the product »leadership«? Everyone talks about customer orientation. Let us be serious about it! Let us focus our attention on the customer. For the customer also decides whether to buy or not. Should we not take this choice seriously? If the customer does not buy it, but rejects it, it is worth nothing. Then it has no reason to exist.

Should we not make leadership much easier to choose and reject? Why not have the leaders elected by the employees? The cheap crack, then the company would be torn asunder by permanent campaigning to be chosen, overlooks the fact that employees are doing just that every day: they choose! *Employees choose by their attentiveness. They choose by their initiative. They choose by their commitment.*

In the power politics between managers and employees the power is in the hands of the employees: employees are possible without managers; but there are no managers without employees. When I see how much motivation is destroyed daily by supervisors who have lost their posts in terms of employee votes, but with barricaded faces struggle to hold onto their authority in terms of position, then there should be no delay in finding another assignment for these people in the company.

Another objection! The managers will only try to bribe their way through. Objection overruled. If the employees participate in the corporate results they will not choose the most convenient boss, but the best one.

For a strong customer orientation of the management it is important to institutionalize other career anchors in addition to »employee leadership«. Similarly, the decision to make someone manager must be revocable without any of those involved feeling any loss of face.

Trial periods and management tasks limited to a specific duration are options. The timing for such increasing flexibility is not bad: more and more people are quite happy to avoid the problems involved in leadership (»Then I can forget about the constant quibbling!«), if they retain their professional or expert career opportunities, medals and awards.

The ideal manager

For decades people have searched for the »ideal« manager, collecting libraries of personality prerequisites – and completely ignoring the fact that managerial effectiveness is dependent on something altogether different: the choice of the employees. For a long time I also took part in discussions about the characteristics of an ideal manager. What they have to be and can do; authentic portraits of heroes … at any rate, a mortal would have a very hard time meeting the requirements in only one lifetime. Nor do they have to. They must – and that is initially independent of any distilled criteria – be accepted by the employees, that is: chosen.

An example of this from another business area. I was consulting a mid-sized company to pick out candidates for field sales positions. Twelve openings were available. The search for the suitable selection criteria nearly escalated into a religious conflict. I tried to find the lowest common denominator that we could start with: »I think the most important characteristic for our new employees will be whether they can establish a relationship with customers.« Consciously throwing the whole textbook on hiring overboard I added: »Let's just forget the criteria and simply test whether the applicant *is acceptable*.« To reflect real life, we picked out seven very different interviewers in our own company – from the head of the business unit down to the man at the entrance gate – and invited each of the applicants to one hour interviews. Without any instructions regarding how they should be evaluated. We asked the interviewers simply to indicated »yes« or »no« – without stating any reasons. We asked them to make their selection. If the applicant received 6:1 yes votes he got the job. I can openly admit that I considered the whole thing like something out of a wild-west show. But to my own surprise, I can say, after three years: this company, in over 40 years of its history, has never used a more successful vetting procedure: with the exception of one, who left the company during the probation, all the other 11 employees hired were just right for the job.

»Please the customer!« – That also applies to managers. Managers, too, must have a positive impact. Or, in hard facts: a management that treats its employees the way they would like these employees to treat the company's customers, could do without a large share of its marketing activities.

Human relationships

When commitment is the focus of corporate culture then leading has a different feel to it. Commitment can neither be generated by structures nor by management control circuits. Commitment can absolutely not be generated outwardly, only facilitated. The chief executive of the pharmaceutical manufacturer Grünenthal, Götz Dyckerhoff: »Leadership must give people the opportunity to experience satisfaction in their work which they accomplish of their own free will for themselves and the company.«

But commitment can certainly be destroyed. We have known for years that the relationship to the immediate manager is the Achilles heel of work satisfaction. This is the decisive point for motivation and commitment. If the relationship to the boss works, all experience shows that the employees are prepared to put up with many irritations in the company.

That is one of the most overlooked principles in management altogether:

Leadership is relationship.

In order to fulfill the leadership assignment the manager needs a vital relationship with his employees. A relationship starts with trust. If you do not trust your employees, your employees will not trust you. More importantly: if you do not trust your employees, then you do not have any.

Highly complex systems cannot be hierarchically controlled without significant losses in speed. If someone wants to act and react quickly in business there is only one means: a relationship of trust. The expertise orientation of the supervisor model, however, directly avoids a relational culture (»You must put more distance between yourself and your employees!«). So, when the question involves employing staff as *backers* and not merely as *suppliers* of a service, briefly: making responsibility available for employees to take, then the relationship to the employees is the primary prerequisite for successful management action. This is testified to by an anecdote about Aristoteles who sent a student home with the words: »I cannot teach anything to him, he does not love me.«

While the energy lines of the employees all come together at the »supervisor« and bear fruit which is identified with his person, the »manager« is more »behind« or »under« the employees whose success is his primary goal. This requires leadership thinking that energetically promotes the development of creativity and the ability *of the employee* and uses it to the benefit of the whole company. The classical hierarchy pyramid is, so to speak, »turned on its head«. That does not mean that there is no longer any leadership. However, the meaning of the work is reinvigorated: employees do not support the managers; the managers support the employees.

Correspondingly, for example, a question considered central in the Toyota corporate culture is: »What can I do for you?« How can I support you? What can I do, to make you more successful? All activities are derived from this question. At 3M the word »leader« is being replaced by the word »facilitator«. The change of labels has little impact, I know. But it can be a first step.

Relationships are two way streets. That means the manager can supply certain personal prerequisites which increase the likelihood of success for their tasks. But ultimately it depends on the vote of the employees. You cannot demand this commitment on the part of the employees for a manager. Commitment can only be voluntarily demonstrated. Employees demonstrate it in a way similar to the way trust is placed in someone, when they choose to place it. But leadership can support this process. The most important point here is:

Create a warm, socially emotional climate.

Even if this initially sounds somewhat strange: the only people who should be managers are *people who can smile*. I do not mean by this the guffaws of plastic happiness which is staged by the always happy-go-lucky managers as reality fitness exercises. I mean the atmosphere of taking people seriously which is expressed in attentiveness, inclination and genuine interest. I mean the sort of empathetic relationship with others which recognizes that employees are also the purpose as well as the means. The basic and unconditional friendly disposition towards others – because you like yourself. You can only like other people if you like yourself.

Leading towards commitment

Delegating responsibility is impossible.

Work creation steps

The situation was clear: the boss was the problem. He completely prevented his employees from seeing their work as *their own* work. He dominated every discussion. He handed down every solution – sometimes even before the problem was clearly outlined. He interrupted staff members, completing and supplementing their sentences. He always put his opinion across as an instruction. »I am open to everything, but we should ...« He changed agendas during conferences, addressing points which nobody had prepared to discuss. He made decisions on his own. – Not only that, he complained unceasingly that his employees did not show any initiative.

As it was, he was extremely careful not to say anything about how he felt in such situations. Otherwise, his approach would be different. It is marvelous to be so important, always at the center of events, on the pulse, in the eye of the storm. Playing fireman, the Saint George mounted on his white horse and galloping off to save the community (or, maybe, to save his own skin?), on airplanes to important negotiations across the globe, faxes by the meter, return calls late into the night, people looking to him, waiting for his decision. All that means: »I am important, and I am doing an important job!« In secret he loves these scenes which prove his indispensability. Then he can accept the price he has to pay for it. Charles de Gaulle is quoted as having ironically remarked: »The cemeteries are full of indispensable men.«

This is not acceptable for companies. This manager is working far below his potential. To put it bluntly: such behavior is a massive breach of loyalty towards the company. For how can people behave as entrepreneurs if the leadership is structured from top to bottom as a command and problem solution hierarchy? As long as managers understand their roles in such a way that their assignment is to solve their employees' problems, the employees will run to their managers with their problems. The boss solves the problem, the employees relax again, thinking: »It worked again«, and the boss complains bitterly about his employees' lack of responsibility.

What can be done? Delegate! is the well-intended advice, however rusty with age. Alright, let us do a little delegation.

Delegating instantaneous-type water heaters

This is how it works: the boss calls in the employee: »Mr. Müller, I would like to entrust this task to you completely. It has to be finished within eight weeks and I would like you to give me a brief progress report every Monday morning. And: no matter what – if you have questions or need help, do not hesitate to talk to me. The door is always open.« Sounds neat. But how many bosses check up on their employee, because they just »happened to be nearby«, to ask how things are going: »How's the project coming along?« Killed by friendly fire: the employee clearly discerns that someone is constantly looking over his shoulder. The translation is: »I may have turned this project over to you, but of course I don't believe you can complete it successfully on your own. That is why, every time we see each other, I ask about it.«

There are few practices quite as demoralizing in the boss-employee relationship as this one. An employee must sense that he is trusted, because trust is a two-way street. It is grotesque to see how many hard core capitalistic companies have written Lenin's words about trust being »good«, but control being »better« onto their banners. Yet mistrust only reflects the intelligence of the disadvantaged. But, without trust, employee commitment does not exist.

»But some employees expect you constantly to look after them!« Do you always do what other people expect of you? Or does this employee expectation feed your hunger for self-importance? If you are concerned that employees really assume responsibility, then you must also let go of this task *inwardly* and not be constantly looking over the employee's shoulder, either indirectly or more or less openly. It is the employee's task and he has the re-

sponsibility to complete it. If he needs someone to talk to about it you are available. But there is nothing else for you to do.

Please the boss

Many managers have learned to delegate, some with greater, some with less difficulty. A few chunks of rock were cut out of the quarry called the boss and »turned over« to the employees (»I would most really like to do everything myself, but there is not enough time...«). The employee takes care of the task and turns in the result to the boss. The boss then assesses the work, since he wants his employees to work to standards he sets.

Such an attitude is not wrong. But it has consequences. Employees learn pretty quick how a job should be performed – in a way which pleases the boss. They spend a lot of time trying to second guess what is wanted. When they do not achieve results, they ask what the boss thinks. Every detail is checked and double-checked. They keep the boss constantly informed (which in the end costs the boss more time than it saves). They sit in meetings and speculate, whether this or that hierarch will »go along« with their solution. »Please the boss« – that is the illness which we have contracted by delegating responsibility. For delegation means: turn over the tasks to others, but make sure that the work is done the way the supervisor wants it done. Farewell, individual responsibility!

It is simply impractical to make one's own yardsticks binding for all others. Managers must learn to recognize the »miracle of being different« (Martin Buber). People will not take responsibility if you try to force unfamiliar benchmarks onto them. In a delegation climate your best employees will quit. Sooner or later. Physically or psychologically. Really creative employees will not play along for even six months. Such a scope is too narrow. That is one of the reasons why so many good people would rather work in small organizations.

Do not tell your employees what best practice »is«. It is in any case only what you consider to be best practice. The employees know best what best practice in their job means. Ask them! What does best practice mean to you? What obstacles prevent you from achieving it? Who can change them? You still have the possibility to negotiate if you have fundamentally different standards.

You need some courage to turn over authority to your employees, and let them do their job the way *they* want to do it. But it is worth it.

»Delegate« responsibility?

If individual responsibility is talked about in business – and »delegating responsibility« is the undisputed management hit –, then a noticeable regression of the employee into childhood cannot be overlooked. The leadership principles of one of the largest German car manufacturers: »The task of the supervisor is to teach his employees to be self-reliant.« This is the language of raising children. Logically it has something of the »Be spontaneous!« paradox about it: a command to ignore the command only deepens the irritating dependence: the recipient can either follow the command or not, but, whatever he does, he cannot be spontaneous.

A major Bavarian bank wants »empowered individual initiative«. Indeed, a powerful word. Certainly well meant, as well. But, sadly, nonsense. Individual initiative cannot be »empowered«. Individual initiative empowers itself. It does not ask for permission. If it needs permission, it is not individual initiative anymore.

The phrase parroted everywhere, »delegate responsibility«, moves, as a result, on the same intellectual level as the manager dream, one could enduringly »motivate« employees to do something that they themselves do not want to do. Formally the boss delegates tasks downward, and more importantly, being up to date, says: »Now you have more responsibility!« – and mutely

reinforces the dependence by saying this. A double message: »I determine when you are permitted to be individually responsible.« That is about as effective as shouting the command: »Relax!« Individual responsibility dependent on God's mercy is psycho-»logically« empty.

Not delegable

I frequently hear you have to delegate the responsibility along with the task. What is frequently meant by this is an odd collection comprising free choice of the means to use and details of implementation plus »I am turning over the responsibility to you!« in case things do not work out. Have you ever asked yourself, and attempted to imagine, what that means: delegating responsibility? Let us consider – as a very representative case – a bank: »Managers ... give employees total responsibility for the tasks they assume.« Does this sentence say anything? Something, which has meaning in terms of action? No, this sentence is empty. One cannot *give* anyone responsibility. People have responsibility for the task the moment they said »yes« to the task. You can subsequently make them accountable if that is important to you. But you cannot give anyone responsibility (from outside) if they do not want to accept it. Responsibility cannot be »delegated«. If your employees do not want to take responsibility on their own, then they will duck it.

Individual responsibility is an attitude.
It cannot be delegated.

Your can delegate tasks, but not responsibility. Responsibility can only be *taken* by employees – if they want it, because they have *chosen* it, if their inward attitudes favor responsibility, no matter what the legal pursuit of criminal responsibility may say. In this sense, responsibility is always individual responsibility. It is the action of the employee. It is a self-empowerment from within.

Of course, as a manager, you can *take away* responsibility: to do that you must take the task away. For example, if errors impend, or the task is executed in such a manner which does not correspond with your expectations. But precisely at this point the precipice is dangerously near. When a situation heats up, managers traditionally tend to *remove* employees from their responsibilities, referring to legal or, following the logic of power, »higher« responsibility of the supervisor. They define the scope of action narrowly. The whole affair is finally classified as a »matter for the boss«. After all, one – »bears the responsibility«. Uh-huh!

This pompous »matter for the boss«: everyone should know that the problem is a terribly important one, that the others who had previously dealt with it were all incompetent and that now the brilliant solution is around the corner. Then, at least, it will be clear, who is the boss in this company. As boss you need only act like this two or three times and you will have produced another Death Valley of individual responsibility.

Thus, leading to promote individual responsibility can only mean:

Leave responsibility with the employees!

Also and especially when difficulties arise. Precisely in such a situation decisions related to »individual responsibility« are reached! Leave responsibility where it belongs: with the person who has been given the task. A major challenge for some managers.

But, in practical terms, what can »let the responsibility rest with someone« mean?

Responsibility for decisions

In a small elitist foundation for the elderly which is exposed to relatively fierce competition for wealthy customers in its location, the care provider, the investment service and the administration sell a package deal »services for the elderly«. The chief administrator, Christiane S. also heads the home. It is customary for the residents of the foundation to show their appreciation for the care they receive from personnel with small donations. These donations were, for a time, always distributed equally among those working as attendants. One day the head of the home received a very friendly note from the relative of a resident and a one hundred mark bill (ca. 50 Dollars) »for the house«. Christiane S. used the money to buy especially nice table cloths, »because then everyone gets something out of it«. At one of the following employee meetings of the attendants Christiane S. was blamed for having spent the money unfairly since 1) the money could only rightfully be given to the attendants for their »care for people« and 2) expenditures such as those for table cloths ought to be paid for by the foundation itself anyway. Both other services then spoke up and submitted their claim to a share of the money, »something which we always had wanted to say.« In a situation similar to a court hearing the head of the home defended her behavior and delegated the decision to the foundation's board of governors. A disaster.

Here we have again the basic problem of organizational irresponsibility: not the company provides the service, but a particular part of it; »we« provide the most important contribution. There is no process awareness, but only department awareness. Moreover, it seems a few long-standing psychological burdens broke open which had been festering for some time beneath the surface. Yet it would be insufficient simply to call the attendants egoists and to argue by whipping up feelings of community. The conflict could have been avoided: the head of the home extends responsibility to the departments. She briefly describes the situation and moderates the decision process. *That* is the role of leaders: to bring about a situation in which all ways of looking at things are respected, and the justified claims of the participants are made transparent and can be negotiated.

Furthermore, where possible, *in advance* of a concrete event, which threatens to detonate the apparently long-standing nasty feelings.

Johannes Kohl, the chief executive of Wacker-Chemie, summarized the on-going process of reducing the hierarchical structure in his company since 1985 as follows: »It is surprising what astonishing results you get if you put the responsibility for decisions into the hands of those with the expertise.« But managers have gotten into the habit of making decisions for their employees. That is an essential element of their self-image. The results are obvious: employees will not take responsibility for these decisions. A quality reviewer who had eliminated his own job and put the quality review back into the hands of the »producers« told me: »Whatever I did was wrong. If I decided to sell the poorer quality products the customer complaints increased. Our people then said: ›You shouldn't have approved this shipment!‹ If I held back the goods: ›Some of the material is really not so bad. We could have sold it. Now we won't get our quarterly bonus. That's unfair.‹«

There are, no doubt many employees who are willing and have always been willing to accept responsibility. Most employees feel responsible for their work, for fulfilling a task, for solving a problem, for achieving a goal. If this were not the case, some companies would not exist at all. A mid-sized building contractor: »My crane operator bought the crane himself. I have had good experience with this. It is then ›his‹ crane. He feels responsible for it.«

Experience has taught me that this feeling is very widespread: »If they would only let us do our jobs.« Such employees can only be discouraged when responsibility is taken away from them. Then the reaction is: »Why should I care anyhow?« What happens then may be similar to what happened at a large furniture outlet in the industrial Ruhr region. There, the furniture purchasing, which had previously been looked after by the sales people themselves, was taken over by a central purchasing office as part of a major restructuring effort. The intention was finally to »get over the hump« in terms of costs. And they did: from then on it was all downhill. Sales plummeted. The sales staff were no longer enthusiastic about the pieces which were »presented« to them by the head office to sell. They had no feeling of pride in these products, little interest and less success. A typical reaction to being stripped of a responsibility.

An unreasonable demand: freedom of choice

However there are, on the other hand, also employees who have the banner of escape fluttering in their minds. These employees are working hard at keeping their bosses hard at work. Furthermore, the bosses work hard at making decisions and solving problems which are not their own. The attempt to avoid responsibility is often accompanied by a self-chosen trivialization: »This decision is a task for management. We are not paid for that.« Of course – they were trained for years to be dependent on the decisions made by their bosses.

Alternatively, the mask of »pretending to be clueless«. The marketing director of a major food business is perplexed: »The employees do no accept any responsibility, they always wait, look to me wide-eyed, hesitate … They never make completely thought out suggestions which are ready for decisions. Then I say: ›Get together with X or Y this morning and we'll talk about it at noon.‹ What is presented at noon is, in terms of substance and form, a big nothing. Most of the time I make suggestions then.« – I know: time is short. But as long as this manager behaves like this the employees will not take responsibility for themselves. They get the help which permits them to avoid working on themselves. The time pressure will grow.

It is difficult to let responsibility rest with people – we sense this all over in numerous projects with semi-autonomous working groups. Many people had their sense of responsibility spoiled in their childhoods. During their 30-40 year careers they have never learned to make decisions and bear the consequences of them. Instead they have adopted the opinions of their supervisors as closely as possible and avoided taking any initiative. One pharmaceutical company provided each of its 150 representatives with annual marketing budgets of 5,000 marks (ca. 2,500 Dollars). One month before the end of the year not a single mark had been requested! Freedom of choice, as in this case, is often experienced as an unreasonable demand. Many employees avoid situations which require decisions because they are not prepared to pay the price of the road not taken or even of failure. When someone relieves them of responsibility, they bounce back with: »But that was wrong!« From employees like these you can hardly expect any quick successes. But what is the alternative? Continuing as before?

Here is a story which may or may not have happened as told. If not, it is well devised: a business unit manager for corporate development was known for his tendency to let responsibility rest with his employees. One day an employee came to him in an effort to cover himself: »I really cannot decide what to do in this case.«

His boss in a friendly voice replied: »If I decide this for you, it will cost roughly DM 12,000 (ca. 6,000 Dollars). I'll subtract it in 12 installments from your salary – for the fact that I am doing your work.« The employee laughed, considering it a joke, and let the boss decide. When he got his next paycheck he wasn't laughing any more.

The employee who does the job is also responsible for the job. There is nothing to »delegate«. All employees must take responsibility for their performance. They must also decided how this job can be best done, which tools they need. They must learn to understand how to make their own decisions and to live with the consequences. Only if each employee is responsible in this way is commitment to a decision possible. A worker responsible for fitting doors at Opel: »I decide when I am finished. If I am not satisfied, everything comes to a halt.« Commitment results from the »yes« to this task, from the feeling of being responsible for decisions.

This kind of letting go does not mean letting employees do whatever they like, ignoring any share in the responsibility and stepping back from exercising any influence. This kind of letting go does not have anything to do with lack of conviction or laissez-faire. On the contrary: it is based on the firm conviction that nearly all employees know what has to be done and that one can only undermine this self-reliance.

Leadership based on individual responsibility as the central value of corporate design is directed much more by *letting* than by *doing*. Not an easy task, as the vast majority of managers are defined by their assertiveness and their »clear decisions«. Are you still under the illusion of the »one single correct« decision which you, rather than your employees, are better at finding?

Do you have no trust in the decisions of your employees? Then do not be surprised that your employees have no trust in you. But for a manager who has understood that there is no single correct answer, leadership can only mean: *do not take choice away from the employees*. Let the employees find their own answers.

Thus, leadership is responsible for providing the framework in which all employees are encouraged and enabled to accept responsibility for their job performance. Willfred Mayer, member of the board of directors at Wilhelm Karmann GmbH: »The art of leadership consists of creating constellations in which the employees who should decide are also able to.«

That means, among other things, an information system so complete that the employees have all the relevant data at their fingertips which is necessary for important decisions. But, most importantly, the employees must know the results of their action.

Even if the results involve problems and difficulties.

Making suggestions

The head mechanic approaches the foreman: »So that is my problem. Could you give me few ideas on how to handle it?« – »Yes, have you already tried …« – »Yup, but it didn't work.« – »Well, then perhaps …« That won't work either, because …« – »Well, then I guess you'll just have to …« – »I tried that three months ago already! That won't work either!«

Recognize the dialogue? The foreman is sucked more and more emotionally into the problem description presented by the head mechanic until he is literally in the »grip« of the difficulties. The pressure to come up with an answer is felt, and the foreman starts to give his head mechanic a few tips. Or will he just keep the discussion short? It is an age old game, played out in companies thousands of times a day. The basic idea is: »Show me the soup in which I cannot find a fly!« The name of this psychogame is: »Yes, but …« and the employees win in three ways: firstly, they get attention. Secondly, they can show superiority by rejecting suggestions (»I'm familiar with that, I know that, I'm better than you!« Thirdly, by soliciting suggestions like this, they can slip out of responsibility, and also rob the boss of time.

Employees often expect a solution. But whoever has a problem, also has a solution. *It is impossible to have a problem without a solution.* If someone comes to you with a problem he always brings with it the resources he needs as well. Often his view is limited, he is hypnotized by the problem and not aware of his options. Usually the employee knows very well what the solution is, but he simply does not want to bear the responsibility for the consequences of that solution, and wants back-up support. But sometimes he only needs someone to talk to, in order to develop a solution in discussion with someone else.

Managers who »know how it's done« in these cases also are convinced there is only one correct solution. They ignore the wide range of possibilities. They are more interested in showing off their own genius than they are in promoting employee potential. They interrupt the creative process of searching for answers which those immediately responsible are involved in. But the price of this interruption is high: suggestions kill commitment.

The rescue worker model

The rescue worker model of leadership as providing first aid, which says that urgency dictates the right approach, is very widespread. This most accurately reflects the basic accident-type character of any employee »attempts«. In addition, it complements the moralizing hiring of irresponsible employees. In sales organizations the rule is: if the field salesman has a conflict or a problem with a customer he runs to his boss, who takes over the matter and clears up the problem with the customer. The effect on the employee is, in any case, negative: maybe he thinks »It worked again« – and remains bereft of responsibility. Or he resigns: »I cannot solve my problems alone.« The effect on the customer: »The little field worker cannot make decisions anyway, I'd better deal directly with the boss.« (And, indeed, many customers then want to have their important discussions with the boss.) The boss feels terrific as the disaster relief agent for P and L, but may also become resigned to the overload of responsibility, complaining soon afterwards about the employees' lack of responsibility. Frequently the boss fluctuates between feeling like the heroic little fireman and the overloaded whingeing repairman (»Everything is left to me!«).

Saving the coal from the fire? You can tell your employees where the tongs and the gloves are hanging, but they should pluck the coal out of the fire themselves. Respecting someone means first and foremost: do not save!

The best corrective for problems and difficulties is to face up to the consequences. For every action there are logical and natural consequences. They are a result of the situation. Logical consequences can be easily identified by the question: »What will happen, if I do not get involved?« Logically natural is repairing the damage or compensating for a defect. Employees experience and therefore bear the consequences for what they have done. If the manager withdraws in this way, *appropriately* and *having thought the matter through,* the logical consequences will release employee learning energy.

Leadership means, as a result, showing employees, that it is in *their* power to solve the problem. Not to do what *you* demand. An end to the symbiosis! Of course – and I repeat this again because it is important to me – you can condition your employees to do what *you* think is right. The more a manager solves problems for the employees, the less they do themselves, the less commitment is in the company. That is neither wrong nor immoral. But then you should stop talking about commitment.

After a seminar, a manager wrote me a letter: »For years I was the champion rescue worker for dependent employees. A short time ago a key account manager came to me with a problem which he had with one of our most important customers. Normally I would have immediately taken over the matter myself, the sales volume involved was too much. This time I didn't. I discussed alternative approaches with my employee but I asked him to decide the matter himself and to resolve the problem himself as well. My employee was shocked at first. Accustomed to reaching for a helping hand, he was initially very unsure of himself. I too felt the temptation to settle the matter in my own way. But he then reached a decision, met with the customer and settled the matter. Later he thanked me for providing him with the opportunity to solve his problem on his own. But that was not my most important success. Much more important was the fact that I had resisted the temptation to act out the old rescue worker routine.«

The same applies to dealing with internal business conflicts. In the hierarchical construction of organized irresponsibility there is hardly any direct communication. Communication takes place mostly through a wall of falling water: because the point is not how to solve a problem but rather to go through the proper »channels«. Demotivation snow balling. In this connection the imputation is that employees are too stupid to describe the situation themselves, explain their behavior, or if necessary, defend it. In the light of commitment, an ambivalent situation: many managers will hold their protective hands over employees, because employees expect that. On the other hand, employees have to learn to stand up for themselves; they can increase their abilities to deal with conflicts. Even today I am still thankful to my first boss for this lesson: if someone complained about me to him he would refer the person to me, his employee: »He is in the next office; he can speak for himself, and he can provide the best explanation.«

Barricaded by solicitude

»Mr. Meier, don't you think you ought to get a few more charts ready for tomorrow's presentation just in case?« – »No, I think I am so familiar with the subject that I can give a satisfactory answer to any questions.« »Oh, I think you had better; the sales manager has the habit of asking unpleasant questions. It would be better to get something ready that you can offer him.« Mr. Meier goes to his office to make a few more charts.

This type of manager decides when the employees are sufficiently prepared or not. They are over-anxious and want to exercise their protective authority. They seem to possess foresight, vitality and experience – and yet hold their employees down in a state of dependence. This, of course, justified by the grave concern for their well-being. But even more importantly this reflects a deficiency in self-reliance, the distrust of ones own abilities in similar situations. This distrust is projected in an irresponsible manner onto the employees. That may flatter vanity, and give the feeling that the employees are no more competent in such situations than themselves, but it leaves the employees in a dependent relationship. The hidden message is: »You cannot see the situation as a whole yet, that is why you will fail if you do not do what I tell you.« In this way the manager takes responsibility away from the employee. Such supervisors replace growth with spoilage because – to be quite blunt – in secret they perhaps fear that any »failure« on the part of the employee could reflect badly on them. For this reason they are prepared to pay a very high price: they weaken any existing independence and rattle the confidence of their employees. In the above case the employee's attitude was: »It will work out.« Now he has the attitude: »It may not work out.« What attitude is more likely to produce success?

On an office door I read a sticker which put it in a nutshell: »Please don't help, the job is already hard enough.«

Managers who consider it important to let responsibility rest with their employees should not provide them with too much »parental care«. We cannot and should not protect our employees too much. They have a right to learn how to master difficult situations.

Leadership resides in the obligation to en-courage courage and self-confidence. This best encouragement is the conviction: »You can do it!« This kind of leadership means withdrawing and allowing employees the space to develop their drive and abilities. Refusing to help and having confidence in the process – and having confidence that the employees can get something of positive value for themselves out of disappointments.

If your issue is to increase the work capacity of your employees:

> *Do not do anything which employees could do themselves.*

Do not solve their problems. Let the responsibility rest with the employees. If you help out your employees every time they get into difficulties then you may be showing your grand abilities and indispensability, but you should not be surprised if the employee feels incapable and irresponsible. Many managers *want* this sort of situation. O. K.! If you are one of them then you really have no reason to continue reading this book.

Role games

Games involving passing the buck are played all over. Not everyone who is looking for help is always trapped in the victim role, and not everyone who helps on occasion is automatically a rescue worker. But in such situations the danger is present of falling into a manipulative role. In the field of leadership and management with its clearly hierarchical structures these roles mesh with each other so closely that rituals of relieving people of their responsibility hardly stand out and are an unquestioned part of the business day.

There are even institutionalized emergency rescue workers: personnel developers, for example, or the absurd Representative Committee for Managerial Staff. The workers' councils too, who, like the unions, at times degenerate to the level of self-citation, because their opponents are gradually slipping away on them, are often not much more than an internal emergency break-down service.

Similarly, the self-image of many managers includes accepting the rescue worker role, if they are not just complaining (»Things just can't continue like this!«) or criticizing (»How often do I have to repeat myself!«) Under the slogan »If they didn't have me ...«

they get involved in anything and everything as well intended, self-righteous helpers, even if they have not been invited: »So, what's up, what's your problem!« They enjoy their reputation of being sympathetic, patient, caring and always helpful. They are always watchful that nobody gets hurt. »I can see you have problem!« They also love to take responsibility for others, without having clearly discussed the matter. »You can come to me *anytime*, the door is *always* open.« Or, with a angelic smile: »I'll see what I can do for you.«

In order to get out of the danger zone of any threatening brotherly love: this is not about those who really need help. But there are, of course, employees who are glad quickly to take advantage of a s-mothering attitude and want to get rid of their responsibilities. If they behave at all then they behave themselves within limits. They complain, instead of fighting: »Whatever I do, it always turns out wrong.« They fluctuate between helplessness (»Today is not my day«) and rebellion (»What else am I supposed to do?«), feel sorry for themselves, describe themselves as luckless (»Why does this always happen to me?«), wait for things to get better by themselves, show initiative only in complaining and are often experienced in moral extortion. They – frequently unconsciously – always look for someone who will assume responsibility for them, and continuously make more or less open offers for a symbiotic relationship. They set an attractive trap: »I'm stuck, please help me«, or: »I cannot call this one, can you make the decision?«

Employees who talk like this want to remain passive and subtly pass the responsibility to the boss. This has advantages for the employees (according to F. Heinzel):

- They do not exhibit any initiative – then there is no danger of offending.
- They do not decide anything – then the danger of a poor decision is averted.
- They take no responsibility – then they cannot be made accountable for anything.

Moreover many managers feel reinforced in their self-righteous rescue worker role, consider themselves omnipotent and walk with pleasure right into the trap: »Do it like this.« Or they even do the work themselves: »Come here, I'll do it for you.« Soon any employee will have discovered the positive value of a »I'm so weak« act – and another sad-faced idler is born.

As managers they will lament their employees' lack of responsibility with the grieving gestures of a cantor and play the pyscho-game of »completely overworked«. But, of course, that is alright. Since complaining gives the feeling of belonging and being important. Do you want to do without this?

This action program is played out in our companies every day, millions of times. The individuals' sense of identity tends to be partially erased; there is no »Here I am. There you are.« There is no negotiation and no agreement which really counts. As managers either strict or benevolent, as employees, over assiduous and with too little responsibility: the restrictive command and conformance roles waste enormous amounts of energy. It is a symbiotic relationship in which the boss and the employee are stuck in complementary roles, hold tight and act as *one* person. In terms of energy, the potential capacity available to the company is thus »cut in half«. The fuzzy role definitions mean that people's own abilities and development potential are neglected. The manager feels necessary, although overworked, the employee pleasantly relieved, although sometimes unjustly treated as incapable. Depending on the relationship, the feelings swing back and forth between good and bad.

Encourage independent search processes

If you are interested in letting responsibility rest with your employees (and you want to do without the thrill of over-responsibility at the same time) then you must challenge your employees to give up their dependence. You can do this by leaving no doubt that the employees will make decisions and act on them. Make yourself available to them for discussions. Your task is to shed light on the logical, natural consequences of their alternatives. You will do better by asking questions than by punctuating your words with exclamation marks:

- What alternatives have you thought of already?
- What, in your opinion, are the advantages and disadvantages?
- What additional information do you need in order to solve the problem?
- What is your recommendation?
- What would happen if you did nothing?

For this purpose you need an attitude which does not classify everything logically into two categories of true and false, but rather a reality full of infinite variety. This type of leadership means: do not suggest anything. Refuse any reverse delegation. But make yourself available for discussions and direct people's attention towards options. Ask questions which *inspire independent search processes on the part of the employee* and focus on resources. Mobilize the static situation: the situation can be influenced, we are not victims of circumstances.

Managers do not have to know »more«. They must not know the solution. Their core competence is knowing how to invite people to reactivate their own abilities, and to face up to the consequences: pointing out options for individual choice, with a clear view of the price which must be paid for each one: »What can *you* do?« In this way you can let the responsibility rest with the employees. The Indian proverb says: »Give the hungry person a fish and he will have something to eat for a day; teach him how to fish, and he will survive.«

Let us take an example from daily office life: an employee is considering attending a seminar but wants to give you the responsibility for the decision: »Do you think that these days will help me?« With the answer: »Of course!« you are not only making the decision but also taking away responsibility for the optimum use derived from the seminar. It is only a small step to the completely desolate practice of those bosses who »send« their employees to seminars (hidden meaning: »There you'll be washed, dried and ironed and, when you come back, you'll feel as fresh as a daisy!«). But if you answer in a friendly tone of voice: »What do you expect?« you leave the answer to the question where it belongs. Perhaps you could ask: »What has been your experience with seminars up till now?« Only in this way does the responsibility for the use of the seminar remain with the participant. Important is: this is not a rhetorical trick, to answer a question with another question, but simply the rejection of a symbiotic over-responsibility which is not appropriate to the situation: how are you supposed to know whether a seminar will help other people?

The fair appraisal will recognize a dark side to this: many employees – possibly weaned of responsibility decades ago – will discount you as »unable to make decisions«; some of your bosses will probably begrudge you the fact that you do not have your employees »properly under control« (usually those people do not ask themselves how *they* would feel if they learned that one level higher executives had opined: »I have got him under control«). If you do not want to pay this price, forget commitment.

The rescue worker is always the sucker

Especially because in companies the symbiotic roles often complement each other so neatly conflicts are often experienced as »dissonance«. A dispute between two employees is especially something which no manager likes to see. As a rule, conflicts are not experienced positively as important indications of developments, changes and with their opportunities for new adjustments, but as a »fight« which someone must »pacify« as quickly as possible, in the same way that fires are put out.

Certainly, as demonstrated above, there are quite a few managers who understand the fire brigade act as an essential element in their on-the-job identity, and are successfully invited to play it by employees: »We cannot agree on how to plan the vacation schedule; what do you think, tell us who you think is right.« The employees get attention and are relieved of their own decision in a very pleasant manner. Thus, many managers slip awkwardly on the banana peel laid out for them. They put on the black robe and, face chiseled and expressionless, play the game of »courtroom«. A psycho-social mine field: if you decide in favor of one of the parties you have a problem with the other afterwards. Prior to this you had no problem. Now you have one. If you decide like Solomon for the middle where, they say, the answer lies, you then have created *two* problems.

Moreover, what you ignore is the fact that each of them believes they are right and is pursuing »sensible« goals. There are no »wrong« arguments. It is impossible to figure out who is right or wrong! The rescue worker is always the sucker. »But I only wanted to help.« Exactly. Your feeling is confirmed that ingratitude is the wage of the world.

Over the wide, wide ocean of opinions, how could it be otherwise, the wave also rolls which declares thanklessness as the price a manager just has to pay. Agreed. But that is not the issue here. That the manager does nothing, so that both employees increase their ability to deal with conflicts: *that* is the issue here. That managers think they have found a privileged access to the truth: *that* is the problem. That managers relieve the two pit bulls of their responsibility: *that* is their failure.

Employees must learn to resolve their conflicts on their own. Do not let yourself be drawn into a fight! Refuse the invitations accordingly: »I am sure that you will find a solution which is acceptable to both of you.« Let the responsibility lie where it belongs: with the disputants. Admittedly, there are exceptions; but it must be also said, they are exceptions. The extreme emergency where the manager must actively intervene is nearly always the result of a practice in which the manager has always let himself be sucked into a dispute, and even intervened without being asked because »civil order is the primary duty of every citizen.«

Managers do not have the right to assume the employees' responsibility, nor may they assume the consequences for their employees' actions. This is all the business of the employees. Do not rob your employees of the opportunity to gain competence in handling conflicts only because you would like to play the role of rescue worker, judge, mediator or deputy sheriff.

For my work as a consultant I have made one thought a guideline for myself which can also be important for leadership:

Do not support anyone who is satisfied not to accept his share of responsibility.

Friendly mitakes

Detours expand your knowledge of the territory.

When Edison made a functioning light bulb for the first time, he told a journalist, that of his 250 previous test bulbs, not a single one had worked: »I learned something from each mistake that I was able to take advantage of in the next test.«

Today, everybody knows that without mistakes there can be no progress, no learning. For it is really an open question whether one can do anything »right« or »wrong« in life. Since the other alternative was rejected, nobody can know what would have happened otherwise. The word »mistake« seems, as a result, only applicable for a very short-term view of things. If we survey a longer period, many apparent »mistakes« often turn out to be the pivotal points of important developments whose consequences for us are positive and useful. As the wise man says: »who knows what it may be good for…« One of the most famous examples of this is certainly the adhesive on the 3M post-its which resulted from the failed search for a high-performance adhesive. The IBM model 360, one of the most built and most profitable computers, is based on the technology of its failed predecessor Stretch. Insulin, the vacuum cleaner, the dynamo – all mistakes. Shakespeare's Yorick knew that the straight path, wherever it went, was always the worst, because it trivializes the »treasure of unused possibilities.«

There *are* no mistakes. I can show you a chair. But I cannot show you a mistake. A mistake is an interpretation, a question of chosen perspective. Goethe's position was: »Tripping moves you forward.« It may be that such a way of proceeding is not very graceful. But nature also makes leaps. Without a certain amount of chaos there can be no self-organization. People who perceive things this way are always winners. Their victories reward them with confirmation, courage and energy. Their defeats provide them with experience and stimulate them to come up with better ideas. Moreover: personal bankruptcies should really be celebrated. They add excitement to life and show that one is in the middle of a growth process. Only obstacles, objections – whether one can overcome them the first time or the third time – help us make progress.

Failure avoiders

Even the mistakes which are made in the company are necessary to set out in new directions. Which does not mean that it would be intelligent to make the same mistake several times. The graffito says: »It is not bad to have made a mitake. It is only bad to make a mitake twice.« Of course: regarding productivity, an error can only arise where we can afford to pay for it. Not all manure is good fertilizer. Nevertheless, deep-rooted prejudices are opposed to a constructive treatment of mistakes in the general corporate culture of »I'm right. You're wrong.«

For one, in nearly all companies, mistakes are treated in an extremely dysfunctional manner. Specifically, as if they had been *consciously* made. Reprimands, wild speculations in response to the question »Couldn't you have avoided it?« and the broken record of justification blues are the results. Often an employee runs a machine worth 2 million marks every day, produces every day an exorbitantly expensive product – and is exposed to massive condemnation if he makes a mistake resulting in a loss of 10,000 marks. Justified?

But mistakes cannot be consciously made. Mistakes *happen.* To you, to me, to everybody. More or less frequently. Strictly speaking, therefore, no reason to blame someone or even to get into a bad mood. This is not the same as a shoulder-shrugging »Who cares?« attitude, but a recognition of the simple fact that mistakes sometimes happen and cannot be made on purpose. A company without mistakes is an inhuman company. Or completely bereft of humans.

The important point: a purposeful mistake is no mistake. It is sabotage. How can one differentiate between a mistake or sabotage? A difficult business. As long as the person involved does not admit to a purposely damaging act, one assumes it was a mistake. But then (I am repeating this because I feel it is important.): no reason to reprimand or to get upset. In cases where too many mistakes happen or if mistakes do not result in improvement, this, of course, has consequences. This employee does not belong in this position. But there is nothing else to say.

Moreover, the increasing turbulence on the markets and increasing risks are accompanied by the need for insurance policies of all kinds. Managers, who openly admit that they must rethink matters or even that they have made mistakes are seen as milk-toasts and weaklings. Almost all the terms which describe the process have a negative connotation or stick out due to their overdramatic character: »admitting mistakes«, »confessing to an error«, »a climb-down from a position«, »not sticking to one's opinion«, »switching sides«. Even the correction of views, the harmless word »change of heart« has in colloquial language a bad after-taste. The archaic ideal of the loyalty of the Nibelungen still has much greater status than acquiring a new insight.

Zero mistakes = zero responsibility

Responsibility is a shy deer. If someone is »held to be accountable«, if they make a mistake, they will do everything possible to avoid the responsibility. The best strategy to avoid mistakes is to avoid responsibility. They run the zero-error program: »Whoever does something, makes mistakes. Whoever does nothing, makes no mistakes, and gets promoted.« (The ISO edict of continuous enforcement of ruinous error avoidance behavior raises the whole matter to the level of a corporate codex.) *Zero-error-programs are zero-responsibility programs.* Who is surprised that in the usual, internal corporate cultures of persecution there is hardly anyone prepared to accept responsibility? Who seriously believes that the employees will act as entrepreneurs if the underlying rule of the game at the company is: avoid errors at all cost! The more people »are held accountable« the more responsibility will dissipate into nothing.

The business economics teaching regarding decision-making makes available the »risk-return paradox«. Even if business is booming and high risks could be taken, in general the safer alternatives are preferred to the riskier ones. Whoever wants to try out innovations and take risks is all too often faced with an »anti-innovation alliance« which generates particular solidarity effects in the pattern of the »not-invented-here« syndrome. World champions in prevention. People are most creative in finding reasons why something *won't work.* But the concrete handling of errors is like the litmus test for the required innovation-friendly corporate culture: without a tolerant attitude towards failures, without the support of unusual, risky projects, there is no high innovation rate! At the Texas steel maker Chaparral Steel, the position regarding the risk of errors is: »How risky is doing nothing?«

Riskless risks

The paradoxical policies of many companies are an obstacle to their employees, especially when they are dealing with mistakes. Most companies prefer a corporate culture which chisels the dimensions »Security« and »Order« into their coats of arms. But at the same time the corporate communiqués and memos are bursting with intrapreneurship, innovation and entrepreneurial action.

Overall that generates a highly contradictory climate which implicitly requires something like »courageous lack of errors« or »error-resistant entrepreneurship« or even »riskless risk«.

But as long as the messages are fork-tongued, many employees will hide out in their more or less comfortably furnished security bunkers and apply their skill to developing risk avoidance strategies, more often than not fully aware of the fact that »being unable to do anything wrong« is the equivalent of »doing something completely useless.« If someone asks, for example: »What time is it?«, the following, highly probable, correct answer could be: »Between 5 a.m. and 12 midnight.« One could, of course, also answer: »It is nine minutes past two«, although it is really already ten minutes past two. It is obvious that the mistaken answer is more useful.

The more you attempt to exclude the possibility of a mistake the less helpful you become. It is reminiscent of the English proverb: »The man who does not make mistakes is unlikely to make anything.« Or, as Peter Drucker says: »To try to eliminate risk in business enterprise is futile. Even the attempt to minimize risks can only result in that greatest risk of all – rigidity.«

That is the way it is: who has never made a mistake, has probably never made enough of an effort. But those who want to avoid losing, have usually already lost: courage, willingness to assume risks – and their self-respect as well.

A problem is no problem

The yardstick for any genuine learning experience was formulated by Karl Popper in a lecture in 1981: »The new basic law is that we, in order to learn, ... must learn precisely from our mistakes. Covering up mistakes is therefore the greatest intellectual sin.« Many companies have, for this reason, recognized that *making* mistakes is not really the problem, but *covering up* mistakes. From psychiatry we know: if someone has a problem, that is no problem. It is the denial that one has a problem that causes difficulties.

In the BMW leadership principles the corresponding thought is: »Everyone may make mistakes – except for the mistake of covering up mistakes to the detriment of the company.« And in »Up the Organization« Rob Townsend almost brags that he called his business partners mainly to inform them of his most recent mishap.

The chip and telephone manufacturer Motorola, for example, which in 1993 with sales amounting to 17 billion dollars made a profit of over one billion dollars, started a company-wide campaign for »mistake tolerance« in 1994. Only an extremely high degree of tolerance towards mistakes, Motorola was convinced, could help individual companies in the United States retain their overall competitive ability in the long term. At Motorola two principles are upheld: »Whoever discovers a mistake is responsible for correcting it«, and: »We celebrate defeats.«

In other American companies there is a ritual which involves announcing the »Failure of the Month«. Whatever one may think

of such exhibitionism: the purpose of the ritual is by no means to parade in public the »flop of the month«, but to take »tolerance towards mistakes« seriously; taking seriously the fact that enterprising efforts also produce failures and that there is a lot to learn from failures. In an environment where mistakes are denied, mistakes are covered up and, therefore, not corrected. Worse still: lies and still more lies must be presented ... until so much time and energy is put into lying and misrepresentation that there is no time left for anything else. The employee in a company culture which tolerates mistakes need not put so much energy into covering up mistakes. They are unavoidable anyway.

Passing the buck

The presumed or actual reactions of top managers to mistakes prompts many managers and employees to prove their perfection under all circumstances. First, the mistake is blamed on somebody else. If the individual's responsibility is quite evident, it is embellished or simply not spoken about. Everyone likes to talk about successes, but we keep quiet about failures. An illusion is created. The English Monty Python actor, John Cheese, related an interesting example of this: »I recall a television documentary in which English and French school pupils were asked about the most famous battles which had taken place between the two countries. As you know, the English and the French are arch enemies who have been eagerly fighting each other for over 1000 years. The English pupils named a long list of battles which were all familiar to me. Then the French pupils presented a completely different list of battles: names I had never heard of before. At this moment I clearly understood that during my whole ten years of being taught English history at an English school I had never heard the names of battles which the English had *lost.*«

If a government manipulates history books they can get away with these »mistakes« for a while. But if a company is led by people who do not value mistakes as feedback from the market and ignore them, they will be breeding a conformist yes-men and yes-women culture, promote people who avoid risks and no longer use mistakes to make course corrections. The system is no longer capable of learning. Within the department, people may talk about mistakes. But it is often mortally dangerous to present mistakes outside the department. The beginning of the end of many companies. Victims of being right.

So if we have a corporate culture which punishes mistakes, the company will drift more and more off course. The chief executive will be like the pilot of an airplane who asks his altimeter: »What's our altitude?« and the altimeter responds: »Which altitude would you like?«

The advantages of fuzzy logic

There really are those characters who, with the help of a reading glass, magnify any mistakes to humiliate others. In fact many managers are downright compulsively obsessed with blunders. The slogan: look for mistakes and produce the individuals responsible. But if every mistake, no matter how small, is carefully registered and sanctioned, the employees cannot develop commitment. The »weak point analysts« among the managers (»Delegate and make sure no mistakes are made!«) are themselves the weak points in a corporate culture which accepts that mistakes happen and which, thus, has a future. Those who, instead of seeing the positive side of employee efforts (»glass half full«), would prefer to hold up their powerful magnifying lens to the faults (»glass half empty«), has set his soul and those of his employees in quick-setting concrete. People who are continuously broadcasting their criticism (in a »professional« manner, of course) regally from their authoritative pedestals should not be surprised if employees *motivated by fear* are the result and the output of the whole system drops below its optimum level. Frederic Vester has proven, that in a fear-free test climate, in response to 100 questions, 90 were answered correctly. If the test persons were made nervous, the number of correct responses to the 100 questions was 50. Fear, so to speak, reduced the problem solving intelligence by »half«: fear makes people stupid.

Do something about it

Instead of bringing charges against employees, I think it is more intelligent to react by *doing something*. The employee knows well and better than anyone else that he has made a mess of things. He feels it more than anyone else, even if he is trying to cover it up. There is no need to make a three-act drama out of it. It will not help anything. Now you can only waste precious energy. The mistake happened. So, to repeat the point:

Don't bring charges – do something about it.

Talk about the mistake together, without any recriminations, analyze the causes together, work out the learning potential jointly. Draw attention to any positive value which the mistake may offer. Concentrate less on the erroneous behavior than on the sort of behavior which would have been appropriate. Direct your questions more towards discovering opportunities to change and less towards finding out how it happened. What can be done *now*? What can we learn from this? How can we prevent it from happening in the future?

Nobody fails gladly and voluntarily. Even if you find this difficult: be especially kind to the employee who made the mistake for a while. Build a bridge.

I can accept mistakes and use them to create something constructive. Mistakes are an opportunity to learn and a free supply of information. Tom Watson, the founder of IBM, it is said, called a young manager to his office who had just caused the company a loss of 10 million dollars. When asked whether he was fired, Watson replied: »What makes you think that? I have just invested ten million dollars in your education.« (Of course, Watson could not have afforded educating many employees in this way.)

Seven times a day

Covering up one's own mistakes, or trivializing them or »passing the buck«: nobody can do this quite as well as a manager because of his position. But the just person, as they say, falls seven times a day: communicating one's own mistakes and poor performance openly (but without being cute about it!) is always a call to be prepared to take risks, to act with courage.

For this is the way things naturally are: every new idea holds in store a possible success *and* the risk of failure... otherwise it would not be a new idea. *Every* person makes mistakes. So what must not occur: that it is a mistake to talk about mistakes. We need instead a basic agreement: being able to discuss these matters *openly*. William Smithbury, chief executive at Quaker Oats, to his employees: »I would like to invite you to take risks. There are no older managers in this company who have not had something to do with a product which fell flat on its face, or with a project which did not work out. That applies to me as well. It's like learning how to ski. If you don't fall, you don't learn.« Only bureaucrats are able to afford to do things right, instead of doing the right things. In increasingly unstable markets speed is often prioritized over prudence, which can lead to a high frequency of mistakes. Quality in this context is indisputably an important dimension of the corporate culture. But if trial-and-error processes are increasingly the basis for rapid-pace management, then some – till now by companies neglected – dimensions such as »immunity from prosecution« and »safe zones« must be more firmly anchored in company policy. Only »high trust« creates the guaranteed protection and trust which are necessary to exceed the limits. In the psychological sense we need more »permitters« in our corporate cultures.

The tolerance for mistakes model

In 1994, in the USA nearly 50 percent of all exports to Germany were in high tech fields; Japan's high-tech exports to Germany made up 27 percent of all exports. In the reverse direction the German export quota for high-tech goods to the USA and Japan was just over 16 percent. The major challenge for the German economy is: how can we open markets quickly with innovative products? Innovative products, processes and services can not be prescribed nor »motivated« out of the blue. Nor can they be directly aimed for– for example, by targeting resources. It is much more important to generate a creative environment in which the No. 1 obstacle to innovation is dismantled: intolerance towards mistakes.

Companies are organizations to combat errors, to find certainty, to eliminate doubt. Escape into policies, escape in the handbooks, escape into the certificates. Dirk Baecker has shown, that companies are increasingly required, however, to reintroduce precisely that deep insecurity into the organization, on whose avoidance the functional ability of the organization has been judged till now. Baecker interprets this development as the »reintroduction of the enterprise into the organization.« That means allowance of environmental irritations within the company. For this purpose we must primarily modify the critical approach to mistakes.

We must set up companies in such a way that the possibility of constructive errors is retained. Back in 1987, Tom Peters demanded that more mistakes should be made, more quickly, how else could anyone learn anything? In particular, we must learn to retain our ability to learn. The ISO movement was looking for the wrong opponents. We need not declare war on mistakes, but on a lack of mistakes. Only mistake-friendliness promotes innovation.

»We make progress from one mistake to the next« (O. Marquard).

From evolutionary biology, which concerns itself with the appearance of »novel« organisms, we know that this novelty, modification, deviation, untried creation will initially be less capable, is a »mistake«. But another combination of external conditions may make this novelty »more capable« in the future. This dual ability of organisms to be susceptible to and tolerant of mistakes makes them mistake-friendly – and guarantees their survival. Evolution, the continuous mutual adjustment and common progress, depends on mistakes. These are systems which accept and promote surprises, deviations and distinctions. Systems unfriendly towards mistakes are practically dead. Can we afford a company which can no longer afford people?

Thus, the situation does not require the right to play with fire between kegs of gunpowder, but requires companies which cannot be set ablaze by a single match. This requires structures which are mistake-friendly. The »leaner« a company is, the more these structures are under threat. Redundancies, the many voices in concert, over-supplies, power balances, the market: all these are mistake-friendly systems. The task of management is to offer reality constructs in which commitment can also be enjoyed again in this regard, without the price for it being too high. In this instance I do not mean that we should not avoid a foreseeable mistake. I am only saying that we will still continue to make mistakes and we will make mistakes precisely where they are not expected nor predictable. No methodical effort offers an absolute protection against mishaps. We must create structures in which mistakes are not too expensive or even deadly. As long as people can learn from mistakes it is helpful to encourage them to assume risks. There is only one mistake which we must never allow: the one which can only be made once.

All the above means a high degree of tolerance towards setbacks; one's own and those of employees. Thus there is one serious (leadership) mistake: not conceding any to oneself or to others. Only the mediocre always work their best.

How can change be introduced?

As is well known, the task of management is to disrupt people who are trying to work. Of course this is done in the name of grandiose rationalizations such as »implementing strategies«, »designing change«, »restructuring«. From »change as an event« to »change as a way of life«. From rigid structures to flexible structures. From hierarchies to networks. From knowledge to learning. Just imagine there were no managers: the processes would flow in a natural, self-controlled manner. Better? Worse? By which yardstick? Management is probably often itself the crisis which it seeks to overcome.

This self-established mission to disrupt also refers to the individual employee. This too must be substantially changed. The type of manager who works on changing people has for years delighted in the complicity of the psychologists. With their bags of tricks they hurry to the rescue with all kinds of employee typologies, needs models, motivation theories. There are the alpha employees, the beta employees, the omega employees who, of course, must all be »treated« differently. I can imagine the managers, how they *analyze* their employees with the handy type taxonomy, similar to military intelligence officers, and then, psychologically sensitized, NLP trained (Long live the partnership!) set out to adjust the employees to their own expectations. »Have no fear! It's only me, your boss!«

Everything is the product of the spirit of one-upmanship. It is the product of »I know something about you. But you don't know that I know that. I am now doing something with you. And you have no idea what's happening.« All this, of course, is only for the benefit of the employee. But what the best is, is decided by the superior field chaplain of manipulation. To paraphrase Tucholsky: if I had a dagger, I would lift it.

But how can one change without manipulating, influencing, without rescuing, leading, without demeaning? What can be done so that the employee says: »I'll do it!«?

For starters:

Avoid reward and punishment.

There is always a certain lack of respect built into any reward and punishment approach. Children are rewarded and punished. I reward someone below me in rank, a subordinate for their »help«. Not for independent contribution which they make to the whole but because their contribution is »for me«. If I, the boss, am the focus of their efforts, then their energy is, so to speak, a »part« of my performance. But how then should they take responsibility for it? By an element of reward/punishment we refuse our employees any feeling of responsibility, that is created solely from the feeling of independent cooperation. Put explicitly: if reward and punishment assume a role, you can say goodbye to commitment.

In a system of mutual respect, the work is done which must be done. In partnerships, each partner makes an independent contribution. Each is responsible for their contribution. They are not working »for me«, but for the whole. Motivation and commitment grow out of the harmony between two people who achieve something *together*, who are cooperative partners. Partnership is what partnership achieves.

You cannot force employees to assume responsibility. Nobody can assign responsibility to someone else, if they do not want to accept it. You can only create the *conditions for the eventuality.* Ask yourself: under what conditions are you prepared to assume responsibility? You know the answer: in an atmosphere of trust, of dialogue, of agreement, mutual support and mutual respect.

But how can change be effected without punishing and rewarding?

Reflect on the following sentence for a few moments and consider whether it has an important message for you.

Criticism does not work.

If that is true: why does criticism not work? Most of you will have the feeling: no matter how »constructive« criticism may be intended, criticism always hurts. Criticism injures. You, yourself, have the best intentions, and now, as before, you consider your behavior sensible and appropriate under the circumstances. Then someone comes along and says: That's all wrong! What right has he got?

Criticism hurts firstly because you have possibly forgotten that all judgements are egoistic. That there are only subjective constructions of reality. You believe that the negative judgement of the other says something »bad« about you, but in fact it reflects primarily the way the person who is judging perceives and evaluates things. Strictly speaking he can only make a statement about how he *experiences* you. Not how you *are*. If he expose his experience and makes it available to you, it is called »feedback«. Feedback says: »This is how I experience you.« It does not say: »You should not change.« Feedback is not a challenge to come into line with the expectations of the feedback giver. *Feedback leaves the choice open.* Feedback stems from the service context. It makes information available to the other person which was not available to them up to that point. It shrinks the so-called »blind spot« in one's self-image because the self-image is then supplemented by an image from someone else. Feedback is thus a potential learning experience.

But when does feedback become criticism? At the point when the other person presumes they are telling the *truth* about you. Then they are no longer saying: »This is how I experience you«, but: »This is how *you are.*« Then they drop the standpoint of subjective perspective. They reserve for themselves a monopoly of interpretation: »I have the right, to criticize you.« They believe they are in a better position to make authoritative judgements: »I know what is good and right.« The critic has the same inward frame of mind as the persecutor who incorrectly assumes to be in possession of absolute, objective yardsticks. In the company, therefore, feedback is, so to speak, »structural« criticism if it is linked with hierarchical power.

Critical futilities

But it is still not plausible why criticism does not work. I would to offer four reasons:

1. Feedback gives the other person the choice to decide what they will do or stop doing. If however you tell someone that they should change in order to please you, you turn them into a loser and you expect subordination. Criticism is demeaning since the power relationship compels them (does not force!) to change in order to meet the critic's benchmarks. In order to retain their dignity, therefore, the person criticized will reject the criticism. Outwardly they will probably conform, and agree in a superficial manner. But what has been won, if the other person conforms? Do you really believe that the other will let this happen to them without taking consequences? They say »yes« and mean »no«, and ensure they get repaid, in secret. A little bit every day.

People are »homeostatic« beings. They find their balance over and over again. If you, because you are boss, discredit employees and compel them to conform, you will pay the bill for it. For they will get back in some way or another. They will find their balance again, rebuild their injured self-respect. By discrediting you. By

cheating you behind your back. By presenting you with the bill on a point so that you do not recognize it *immediately*. But you notice it indirectly – when productivity drops, fluctuation increases, absenteeism rates increase, whingeing circles are established, rates of illness reach record levels. You always pay the price. For every credit entry booking there is a debit entry. You may not see it immediately, but you can see it reflected in your profitability.

> *Every solution to a problem which someone discredits or discounts, is a non-starter.*

2. If you criticize someone, i.e. exploit your power, you invite them to justify themselves. The person criticized will attempt to improve their position. For this purpose they will tell you a »story«. In this story they will look better and reduce the maximum of truthfulness for the sake of the excuse. This is called lying. When you uncover the lie, you complain again about a phenomenon for which you share responsibility.

The same thing happens, by the way, with children: if you accuse children of something, they tell you a fantastic story which is colored by the necessity of wanting to look better. That is also alright. Even in the Bible it does not say: you must not lie. It says: you must not carry false rumors ..., and that is something else. The issue is never one of truth, but always of truthfulness.

3. Only the learning person can decide for himself where his learning problem is. You can start the process from outside, but employees must choose for themselves. Giving an employee a target for change does not work because it is not a »learner's« goal (which comes from inside) but a »teacher's goal« (which comes from outside).

Criticism and learning, therefore, do not fit together. As long as the reality-construct view is not recognized, as long as no heed is paid to the fact that we can only make statements about our experience, but not about the truth, there will be no learning organization. The purpose of criticism is to produce the guilty, not to solve problems. Criticism always creates losers.

The important thing, however is: because I resist the power aspect which is experienced as painful, I may not hear important messages whose substance is feedback. So I will never change myself. At best I will adapt and, subsequently, ensure I get repaid.

4. Criticism is negation. It says: do *not* do something! But that »not« is hardly perceptible by consciousness. Our brain – based on every thing we know about it to date – is apparently bad at processing the »not«. It is, for example, hardly possible *not* to think of something specific. If someone tells you not to think of a tree, the first thing you think of is a tree. Our brains erase, so to speak, the negative sign in front of the object. So, if you do not want to do something, you expose yourself to the continuous influence of an act which you have just decided to avoid. You can be pretty sure that, in this way, you are amplifying the action. For this reason, one's own resolutions, *not* to do something, or the directions to

others, to stop doing something, usually fail. Without the elementary prerequisite of a *positive* expectation the chances of change are therefore slight. But that is the object of negotiation, not of criticism.

At this point I would like to refer back to the context of commitment: you have not been created in order to meet the expectations and gain the approval of others. If you are criticized: never justify yourself. *People who justify themselves, demean themselves.* Even if you are under pressure: take responsibility for what you do. Resist the temptation of attempting to wash your hands of the matter. If you are in the wrong, you do not need to justify yourself; and certainly not if you are in the right.

Even in the case of feedback, you can choose whether it contains a piece of information which you up till then had not had at your disposal. But which, possibly, you could make important for yourself. But you need not automatically adapt the other person's assessment. And if you have chosen to work together with the other person, you will find a way which is satisfactory for *both*.

Is that too idealistic? It is simply practical.

For both parties.

Criticism versus confrontation

Managers tend simply to ignore their own contribution to the behavior of employees. Furthermore, they generally do not consider at all that it may have something to do with them. It is questionable whether one has to go as far as Willfred Mayer, member of the board at Wilhelm Karmann GmbH: »If the employee becomes a disruptive factor the performance of the manager must be reviewed.« But certainly this sentence contains an accurate insight into something which is much too frequently overlooked.

There are many reasons why an employee may consistently underperform:

- The manager failed to set up a feedback culture in which management and employees describe their mutual experiences on a regular basis. The problem is put up with until a remedy is nearly impossible. Many managers shy away from disputes and miss the point at the time when the problematic behavior still could have been influenced.
- Expectations and yardsticks are not correlated. It is necessary that you *discuss standards* with your employees: what is important to me? What is especially important to me in our cooperation? What should be avoided at almost any cost? In the face of what kinds of behavior am I especially sensitive? Invite your employees to give you the same input from their perspective. Do not believe that you already know that is important to your employees in daily contact. What you »understand« or believe you have recognized, are merely your own explanatory models, your speculations about other people's motives. It is better *to ask directly*.
- The employee has insufficient qualifications and receives inadequate additional training; responsibility rests (also) on the shoulders of the manager.
- The employee, with his abilities, is in the wrong job; responsibility rests (primarily) on the shoulders of the manager.
- The employee is notoriously work-shy; (complete) responsibility rests on the shoulders of the manager who either hired the wrong person, did not intervene soon enough or did not have the courage to fire him. Especially on this issue we in business have an enormous resoluteness problem. (The sort of compromise summed up in the words »We are all human!« stinks.)

  It is of course hardly a matter of accepting the behavior of an employee which, in your view is not acceptable. Feedback which allows the other person the choice is one thing. But what should be done if the issue is no longer feedback but the fact that for you the situation has become intolerable? You have a right to change the situation, if you do not like it anymore. The most irresponsible thing you could do is to avoid a clear dispute, to put up with the conflict, to delay before arranging a discussion as a last resort. A distinct addiction to harmony, the inability to deal constructively with conflicts and the everything-under-control mentality silence many managers in situations where what should be said is: »I am unsatisfied with your performance!«

Partner-like leadership is repeatedly confused with laissez-faire, love, peace, harmony and penetrating happiness on all levels of the business. But not even in Cologne, which loves its carnival season, are the people in a roaring good mood all year round. Teeth-grinding composure and the fist in the pocket won't help anyone – least of all, you. Do not carry around your negative feelings for long, it is psychosocial pollution of your inward environment (unless you want to join a society of the victims of stomach cancer). It cannot be denied:

Self-respect comes before respect of others.

Only if you genuinely admit to your feelings, your interests and your ways of looking at things, only if you respect yourself, only then can you also respect others. If you destroy your self-respect, e. g. if you remain silent when the situation calls for saying something, you are no longer capable of respecting anyone else, or of any constructive interaction with others. Nobody gets anything out of your acting as if you think everything is alright. Have the courage to tell it like it is. It pays.

What can be done? According to the policy »Do something about it!« it is important to tell the other person clearly, and as soon as possible, that you do not agree – without accusing him of anything, producing a loser or destroying the relationship. Crucial: *the atmosphere must be right*. Under pressure this does not work.

I call this activity *confrontation* (although I do not like this term, I just do not have a better one). The differences between criticism and confrontation can be summarized as follows:

Criticism		*Confrontation*
person	–	problem
general	–	specific
blame	–	change
past	–	future
own advantage	–	common advantage

Below I develop both approaches as ideal types, and, in individual cases, exaggerate in order to identify the basic differences. Often there is very little separating criticism from confrontation.

Person – Problem: criticism tends to concentrate on personality characteristics and character traits of the other person. Criticism casts a bad light on the whole person. Criticism says: »This is how you are.« Confrontation, on the other hand, says: »This is how you behave.« Confrontation concentrates on concrete action which presents a problem in the eyes of the other person. It prefers the first person singular: »I have a problem«; it does not say: »You are a pea-brain.« You state clearly to your employee how you feel. You say: »I feel annoyed.« You don't say: »You're impossible.« One is informative. The other is abuse.

General – Specific: confrontation is to the point and occurs quickly. You remain focused on *this* point. »Here and now« the point is to solve this specific problem.

On the other hand, criticism tends to generalize. To increase the pressure to conform, the negative experience is expanded into a broad generalization. Popular phrases are »always«, »never« or »typical«. »You never …« Very often the critic feels the right to generalize since he has been observing the employee's criticized behavior for a long time, kept silent, and secretly kept tab and set a trap: »If he does that *one more time* …«, and snap!, caught again. The victim walks unaware directly into the trap and is completely confused when the critic alleges: »You *always* …« Since the victim is not aware that he *always* … This psychogame is called: »Now I've finally got you where I want you« and is a popular social game in our internal business persecution cultures. Halloo!

Blame – Change: criticism does not want to change anything, criticism wants to press charges. Criticism wants people to throw ashes over themselves. Its essence is blaming people. By discrediting the other person the critic implicitly makes himself look like the better of the two. Morally he feels in a better position and believes to have more right to belong to the community.

On the other hand, confrontation wants change, wants to solve a problem. It is not interested in establishing guilt and justification. The purpose is to optimize an unsatisfactory situation, not to make oneself look better. It means openly stating when performance drops, problems are avoided or even rules of the game are infringed. Precisely on this point is vigorous action urgently advisable.

Past – Future: criticism rolls around in the muck of old issues. It keeps an accurate record of mistakes made in the past and now adds them all up. High noon is at hand. It uses all its energy on the background to the problem … while confrontation concentrates on alternative solutions. Figuring out old, dust-covered, cause-and-effect riddles is not what confrontation is about. It looks forward, wants to bring about an improvement for the future.

Own Advantage – Common Advantage: critics are interested in expressing their negative feelings, in establishing their view of the world as »correct«, but primarily: in securing their own advantage. All critics want their own advantage to the disadvantage of someone else. On the other hand, confrontation is concerned not to endanger the cooperation between two partners. For cooperation the »relationship« is at stake. It would like to preserve the relationship by achieving the common advantage. It asks: »Where is the point at which the matter is settled for me but which is also agreeable to you?«

Criticism is easy. Most of us have been constantly practicing this act since our childhood. But criticism destroys commitment. Confrontation is difficult. Like all leadership. It requires discipline, the deeply introjected knowledge of the subjective perspective and the equally deeply felt respect for the otherness of the other person. But only this respect can retain the other person's commitment.

Assessments

The desire for change requires an assessment. For this reason here is something on the subject of »performance reviews«.

There is a yearning for objectivity – but there is one reality. It is called subjectivity. Only the perfectly clear conscience of thoughtlessness can deny that each person »produces« the employee which he thinks he is merely registering. The performance review of an employee illustrates primarily the characteristics and perspectives of the reviewer, not of the person whose performance is being reviewed. When we try to establish the reality about the other person we only find ourselves. We do not discover the employee »as he really is« but as we have created him.

So, all reviews say more about the reviewers than about the person being reviewed. Simply put:

Every assessment is autobiographical.

So, whatever someone says about you, it is *his* truth, but not *the* truth. Terry Cole-Whittacker has expressed this very succinctly: »What you think of me is none of my business. It's your business.«

Read the performance reviews about your employees as assessments of yourself – and you will obtain interesting inputs.

Is this reason enough to throw out the whole system of performance reviews and coaching discussions? I think not. For on the other side of the scale there are also significant assets. However subjective assessment may be: reviews, judgements, and verdicts occur non-stop. One way or another. What is more, the application context of the performance reviews in an organization is by no means subjective, but rather a *matter of fact* and of consequence for the individual: these reviews determine careers, control salaries, set promotion plans into motion, even initiate the dismissal of a co-worker. They are no trivial matters. For this reason I feel it is simply fair to be open with employees. A few tips may be helpful:

- Assume an inner attitude of a strictly subjective view which does not discount other opinions, observations and benchmarks, but grants them equal validity. Do not consider the way you perceive the employee as the truth.
- In all the handbooks about performance reviews there are tips like these: »Admit that you may be wrong.« No! In your judgement you cannot be wrong. (Unless you consciously lie or you are lacking information.) You have the right to see your employees the way you see them. Do not gloss over anything. Sparing people is a disservice. *Explain* your judgements, but do not justify them. That employees experiences their behavior differently than you is natural. Reach an agreement on experience differences as mutual observation and action obligation (goals) for the coming performance review period.
- It is demeaning and laughable to grant the employee the right to a few lines for an »opposing view«. The employee *can* not experience his performance and behavior as you do. It is impossible.
- Read employee performance reviews as feedback to yourself! You obtain interesting information about how you perceive, your values and perhaps also to what extent you are responsible for the other's behavior.

Reason enough to think over judgements which can be more like games of chance. Regarding the »truth« contents of assessments, you are better off weighing a personnel file than reading it.

Commitment to agreements

> *A commitment is neither good nor bad.*
> *A commitment is a commitment.*

The favorite game of managers is at the same time the most futile: wanting to change employees. It goes under the absurd motto: »You must change, so that I feel better.« But the other person does not respond. People are not trivial machines which move at the press of a button. The »human« system can be affected by external influences, but it cannot be controlled. People only change *if they themselves want to change.* Development cannot be ruled out. But no manager can »develop« the employee.

Employees are the way they are. It is a waste of energy wanting to adapt other people to one's own needs. The question for managers can only be: what consequences can be drawn from »The way the person is«? This is related to the organizational environment, the working conditions, the performance options. But that is not my subject here, rather the necessity of explicit agreements in the manager/employee microcosm.

Negotiation

Whether companies – in terms of commitment – can really be reinvented depends on whether people can contribute. That they have the experience of being personally needed with their talent, their involvement and their interests. That they experience that it is practical and effective to participate. Only people who can contribute *something* and *themselves* remain on stage. No boss has the power to force employees to accomplish tasks well which they do not agree to. People do things well that they want to do. People do not do things well that they do not want to do.

But what is »well«? Performance depends on expectations. How the actually achieved results compare with the expectations is the decisive factor contributing to whether something is evaluated as a success or failure. In general these expectations are thought out top down, for example: »The employees must know what is expected of them.« I have shown elsewhere how expectations arise and the kind of power to control responses they possess. In an accountably responsible company, where the focus is not on conforming but on commitment, expectations are not decreed, but negotiated.

Everything can be negotiated! – This is common currency between partners. Everyone has the right to have expectations and to put them into words, both managers and employees: »I'll go east, because I'll go to the beach«, and: »I'll go west, because I'll go to the beach.« If you, as a manager, precipitously say: »That cannot be negotiated«, then you have killed the living relationship between you and your employee on this point. Dead silence is all that is left of it.

It is simply more practical, to flow along *with* the energies of the employees, instead of fighting *against* them. It is better to control the natural flow gently than to build dams and levees. If, for example, I argue in seminars in favor of negotiating exception rules, then the objection is frequently raised: »Where will that lead us?« – »Then anyone can come!« – »Then we will set a precedent!« Although we have known from the natural sciences for decades that a living organism that does not allow any exceptions is already dead. It is no longer capable of adjusting flexibly to changing environmental conditions. But we need both a leg to stand on *and* a leg to move if we want to make progress. This flexibility, this individual responsiveness to other people, the inclination towards enabling, that is the most important factor. Shshsh! Now comes the big secret of leadership:

Why not?

Why not? Most managers have the attitude: »Yes, but…« They see themselves primarily as preventers, as guardians of the rules, as police officers, as company border guards. They reflexively and rapidly fire off any number of arguments why something *will not* work, instead of examining even once, whether it perhaps could work. »What could we do to make it possible?« – That is the »Why not?« attitude. That is the attitude of the enabler and not of the preventer. (That also applies to this book: I would like this book to be read with the »Why not?« attitude instead of the »Yes, but…« attitude.) Why not… e.g. negotiate exceptions and, if necessary, reverse them again? Is not every one of you worth an exception?

Only by means of the »Why not?« do we use in negotiations the opportunities which are offered by conscious cooperation between self-reliant employees.

Agreement

Whenever I hear a manager say: »I decided…«, I hear two things: firstly – it will either not work or, if it does, only poorly; second – the manager leads an exhausting life. An important psychological displacement effect has been familiar for years: when top-down decisions are made, the employees always look to why it *cannot* work; they look reflexively at what is inadequate. People who believe they must make all the decisions alone have often cut themselves off from their employees. That is neither good nor bad. But it has consequences. What you get in return for this is, at most, efforts to conform. Maybe all you need is the conformance efforts of your employees. But then you should forget about self-reliance. But what you will never get is – commitment.

On the other hand: an agreement is an agree-ment. It is not a decree. Not a target. Not a top-down decision. It is neither laid down in an authoritarian manner nor democratically elected, it is the result of jointly developed way of looking at things. It is achieved using an opposing current procedure. This procedure has only very little in common with the cooperative management style. (This begins, as you know, with an authoritarian decision about which decisions the employees may answer independently within established guidelines.) An agreement culture has simply to do with prudently calculated cleverness. For the only agreements which are durable and binding are those in which the partner really had a say. Agreements which are not like this, are not agreements.

What applies to international law, also applies to companies: agreements are only worth something as long as they seem useful to all parties. Correspondingly, agreements only have binding authority if they do not turn someone into a loser. They must be *winner-winner-agreements*. These mechanics have been sufficiently described elsewhere. Important is: if you, because you are the boss, get your own way 100 % during negotiations you ought to be concerned.

The hardest hitting arguments for a winner-winner agreement is *long-term self-interest*. If you only pursue short-term joint interests, if you can change employees like you change shirts, it may make sense to take advantage of others; at most, there remains a question of individual morality. But if you work with your employees for a longer period of time, then turning them into losers is simply impractical. They will somehow get their own back: people always find their balance again! The energy and quality of the cooperation game sinks. If you believe that making agreements costs too much time, then please consider how much time it costs when you do not include the employee. It is much more intelligent to look for advantages for both sides: to find the point at which both can sincerely say »yes«. Only then do both partners feel well; only then do both partners feel obliged; only then is the essential prerequisite fulfilled for an additional, qualitative step: the step to commitment.

Commitment

William Gore, founder of Goretex, who died in 1991, wrote: »Productivity results from commitment, not from instructions.« I described what commitment is in the chapter »Will«. Commitment is, in this sense, a real mental step beyond the agreement.

For the following example please assume that both negotiating partners have achieved an agreement after honest negotiations, in which both have climbed down from their maximum demands (I am not considering here solution possibility C which cancels and preserves some elements of alternatives A and B in a synthesis). A compromise, therefore, which – considering the daily business decisions – you frequently make do with for practical reasons. What happens then? All too frequently both partners subsequently moan about *what is missing*. About the bit of the ideal that they did not achieve. Especially at the moment when something goes wrong and the nagging starts up again: »If I had only managed to get this point accepted …«

Precisely here is the qualitative leap to commitment. *Commitment is a 100 percent »Yes!« – to a 70 percent agreement.* Commitment says: »I'll do it!«, although some needs remain unmet. Commitment does not focus on what is missing but on what is possible. Commitment does not dwell on inadequacies but sticks to its word. Commitment is a *promise*.

This is sensible against the backdrop of the following consideration: I chose not to play my game alone, but rather together with my employees. I will only like playing the game as long as my employees also enjoy playing the game. If they lose interest in the game, the quality of our shared game will sink. That is why it is practical and in my own interest to let employees be winners as well. That means sacrificing a part of my ideal expectations in favor of the shared game – but then not to complain about it but to recognize it as part of the game. And to give the agreement a 100 percent »Yes!«.

It is therefore apparent that one cannot »commit« anyone. Commitment is like trust. You can only give it. You cannot demand commitment. The words are: »We agree with each other«, not: »You agree with me.« But you should still ask whether the other gives his commitment to an agreement. If not, continue to negotiate ... until you can both completely agree.

Or do not make an agreement! If you do not reach an acceptable solution for both parties, agree not to reach an agreement. »Let's agree to differ.« If you frequently do not get as far as commitment, you should ask whether you want to continue working together. But if you act as if there were a commitment, because you believe you *really ought to*, than you are doing nothing more or less than preparing a breakdown of the commitment.

Of course, the possibility must exist to renegotiate commitments, in case conditions drastically change. If the manager and the employee really cooperate in dialogue there are no surprises either, if the employee renegotiates. That can lead, of course, to frequent renegotiations in turbulent markets. So if you make agreements closely related to market events, do not make their terms overly precise and narrow.

Commitment is an attitude. A »goal« is something else: you can have the goal of becoming the market leader within one year, and know that that is unrealistic. You can only make a commitment for an agreement which contains a realistic increase in market share. I know one company that with their current 250 million marks (ca. 125 million dollars) in annual sales have set themselves the goal of achieving sales volumes amounting to one billion marks (500 million dollars) by the year 2000. You can have such a goal. But nobody can make a commitment to it. That would be tolerable. But unfortunately this company is creating unnecessary problems for itself: a goal like this dodges the fragile beginnings of a commitment culture. Because this goal is unrealistic from the point of view of the employees, and greeted with a smirk.

The rules are thus:

1. Never enter a commitment if you are not certain you can keep it.
2. Only commit yourself to agreements which are important to you.
3. Write down your commitments.

The worst thing that can happen in a commitment culture is the victim routine: »I put soooooo much work into this project, but it just didn't work out.« Therefore: it is the responsibility of the employees to renegotiate immediately if they – for whatever reasons – cannot keep to the agreement. When this point is clear, the employees can control their own work. The employees work in *their* company. Control is superfluous. Logically thought through, in a commitment culture which is really taken seriously, no agreements are broken.

The basic rule of commitment culture is therefore:

Keep your commitments.
Always!

Commitments are neither good nor bad. They regulate the cooperation between people. If you take your obligations seriously, others will do the same. If you break your commitments, others will break theirs as well. You said »yes« to this commitment. It is not important to keep a commitment because that would be morally correct or because it raises your reputation in the eyes of others. But to protect your self-respect.

The marketing manager of a large German brewery told me the following story: »On a business trip I had a few hours stopover in Istanbul before the next flight. I wanted to visit the bazaar and took a taxi. The taxi driver let me know that he would also like to bring me back to the airport. So we agreed on a place and time to meet. About 10 minutes before the agreed time I was at our meeting place. Every minute a taxi stopped to offer me a ride. Although the temptation was admittedly great, I waited patiently until the agreed time. And, as I might have known: my taxi driver didn't show up. I waited another five minutes then I took another taxi. On the way to the airport I first reproached myself: how could I be so terribly naive? But then I realized that I had done the right thing: for my own sake. The point was not to do the taxi driver a favor. The point was: I honor my agreements.«

People who break their commitments weaken themselves, feel an inner self-depreciation: I am not capable of making and honoring agreements. I cannot have confidence in myself. Such a person cannot trust others either. It is very difficult to believe someone when you know you would have lied in their position.

The credibility crisis

Corporate statements do not run into difficulties because they are criticized, but because they are taken seriously.

- »It is completely unimportant, when and where you work. The only thing that counts with us is results.« Said the boss to the new employee who had just been hired. Fourteen days later he meets the new employee in the corridor: »We hardly ever see you here!«
- »We want employees who have the initiative and courage to make their own decisions.« A statement from the corporate guidelines. If the employee is then courageous and something goes wrong, he gets chewed out: »What were you doing, sticking your neck out so far?«
- »Dialogue is our leadership style!« The overriding leadership rule of a German pharmaceutical manufacturer. Decreed top-down by the Board of Directors. Decisively unilateral. The form says that the substance is a lie.

I would like to call your attention to experiences which are described colloquially (and appropriately) by many employees and managers as »schizophrenic« and which are especially suitable to illustrate Burkhard Sievers' diagnosis: »Most of our institutions feature a characteristic split between ... their binding myths, on the one hand, and the real experience of their members, on the other.«

In particular, companies which have affirmed the idea of corporate culture have very frequently fallen into the trap of paradoxical mismatched programming, which blurs the distinctive features of the coveted corporate image. The collective corporate psyche is frequently programmed, unintentionally, (but sometimes also: either on purpose or with criminal negligence), to include contradictory signals – and provokes serious inner conflicts in employees: you can try to guess what was really meant.

There are open contradictions between the corporate guidelines and other rules; hidden contradictions between the corporate principles and workaday reality; the company's reward behavior speaks a different language than the proclaimed morality: a manager completely lacking in social skills is promoted to the top-floor while the corporate principles rank »communication skills« as the most important cultural value – employees who want to be good employees are constantly faced with two possible yardsticks for measuring their own performance. The primary message is: »Do as I say, not as I expect. But also do as I expect, not as I say.« Decision neurosis as daily experience: you do not know whether to pull out your hair or simply give up.

Double bind

Gregory Bateson coined the term »double bind«. Briefly, he used this term to characterize the phenomenon of two, mutually exclusive messages, both of which the recipient cannot carry out. The paradoxical situation arises that you follow the message when you do not follow it. That is exactly what many people experience in our organizations: they always have the feeling that they are not doing the right thing. »Whatever you do, it's wrong.«

In this regard, I am only referring to a very limited extent to the polarities clearly described by Oswald Neuberger as the »dilemmas of leadership«. There are nearly always different, justifiable leadership principles which compete with each other and, therefore, must be weighed one against the other. For example between »employee orientation« and »task orientation«. Daily, unavoidable, so not really anything unusual.

My interest lies primarily in corporate messages which mutually exclude each other. My thesis is, that many companies have maneuvered themselves into a communicative dead-end. They have generated a *message crisis* which all too often creates a working climate of quiet resignation, or worse, withdrawal, and demotivation in the face of unbearable conflicts. A credibility crisis. The common practice of issuing a corporate culture as if it were a decree, more or less overnight, rather like dropping a bomb, is the primary cause of double binds. Let us take a closer look at several of them.

Entrepreneurs without risk

In the branch office of a major bank several loan officers were fired because they had exceeded their credit limits. But at the same time the new corporate guidelines challenged employees to think enterprisingly: »Take risks!« The reaction of the employees: play it safe in every way. But for this degree of security they needed more time; there soon were not enough working hours. They produced less; involvements with potential repayment difficulties were not accepted at all … which, in turn, intensified top management's call for greater readiness to take risks.

»Our employees think and act as entrepreneurs.« These words can be read in the guidelines of a major German company in the building materials industry. But precisely this company has an extremely detailed book of rules. What is more: the most important entry in the unwritten company film script is: »If you make a mistake, it's your neck!« Case examples in which a mistake meant the end of someone's career circulate by the dozen as unconfirmed reports. In the employee's experience on the job, this side dominates: In case of mistakes, no quarter will be given. The results are clear: employees are irritated by the two irreconcilable messages, even three »Act as entrepreneurs!« and »Follow the guidelines!« and »Avoid mistakes whatever the price!«

The situation turns completely grotesque if, then, the managers complain that the employees do not make any use at all of the decision-making latitude granted them for entrepreneurial practice. All they do is play it safe and have everything counter-signed. They are not ready to assume risk.

But is that surprising? It is obvious that a corporate culture intolerant of mistakes generates opportunism, conformism and irresponsibility. Tom Peter's statement on this point can be endorsed: »Nothing is more contradictory than a conservative chief executive officer who demands courage and the willingness to assume the risks of experimentation.«

It is really pretty grotesque to see that, on the one hand, in these days of turbo-management, people want a high-trust culture with

rapid follow-through and the corresponding readiness to assume risk, while, on the other hand, zero-mistake campaigns thunder over the heads of the employees. On the one hand, people dream of learning companies, while a failed project means the unspoken hard fact of a destroyed career. On the one hand, people groan about the innovation and creativity lead of the Japanese, on the other hand, any and all initiatives are strangled by guidelines. On the one hand. On the other hand. This is the internal structure of the double bind: the ambiguity of the undecided, of the eternal not only but also. People who do not occasionally lose their minds under these conditions have no minds to lose.

Competitive cooperation

»I frequently have the feeling that the only thing which my team colleagues find really interesting about me is my failure.« These words of a young team leader – spoken around midnight, a time of day which is no doubt conducive to honest self-examination – reveal a structural conflict which rattles the business community to the marrow and generates many different sorts of critical situations. Demonstrating teamwork is definitely a necessity in markets whose complexity can only be mastered adequately by bringing together expertise scattered about the company. If – unobscured by any doubt – the trumpets did not continue their fanfare of »Competition stimulates business!« A confusing, destructive pattern:

- »Demonstrate team work! – But get your own way!«
- »Be cooperative! – But thwart your competitors inside the company!«
- »Identify with the whole effort! – But only your individual performance will be rewarded!«
- »Serve the interests of the community! – But optimize your self-presentation, after all people have to evaluate you, too!«

Many team formation activities fail due to the fact that the hierarchical bottle-neck or other situations of artificial scarcity also finally turn even the most suitable team player into a competing opponent. Managers will hardly work in teams if the company continues to reward individualism, the ability to get one's own way and departmental egotism. The hierarchical pyramid is a structural force compelling employees (not necessarily by individual intention!) into competition. For one winner automatically produces three to four losers whether wanted or not ... something which, in some situations, is easily »forgotten« but which reappears at the very next meeting. A spiritual loose contact.

Morton Deutsch has convincingly shown that trust under conditions of competition is nearly impossible. The manager must therefore compete without appearing to compete. He must pretend to be cooperative. Even more: during the performance review he even competes with others in the cooperative behavior category. (This can only be cleared up by the chaos theory.) The behavioral conflicts are preprogrammed: masquerades and forked-tongued messages. Promoting communication by staging a performance.

Some companies see the dilemma. They then refer to »exaggerated« competition, make individuals responsible for something which is structurally related and apparent. They handle this dilemma in such a way that they superficially promote cooperation by means of all kinds of slogans – and quietly tolerate competition, in cases of appointments even preferring those by a majority who »have teeth«, who can »get their own way«, but most importantly who are »not too weak«. The encouragement of cooperative behavior may be raised to the level of the moral maxim – but hard facts are rewarded. »Develop employees!« may be listed in nearly all modern management curricula, and there are innumerable training programs on the subject of »communication and cooperation« – but in the evaluation system this skill in particular remains all too often completely forgotten.

A concrete example from business life: many companies have difficulties introducing partially autonomous teams. They blame in general the inadequately cooperative attitude of the employees responsible for the transitional difficulties. They had just not learned yet how to take responsibility cooperatively. The competitive conditions, within which the fashionable cooperation game is played, are walled out. But they are what reward the behavior and, to this extent, condition it. It is barely possible to establish a feeling of community with someone who in fact is my rival.

Illusory interpretations

At present a hierarchy-free, major corporation without internal competition is barely imaginable. Whether it ever will be – that is not at issue here (but perhaps it is simply that my imagination is not creative enough). There are certain paradoxes which we will not escape. Oswald Neuberger even called attention to the fact that this is the prerequisite for the leadership role. In plain terms this ability is called »ambiguity tolerance«: the ability to put up with ambiguity; balancing conflicting interest, both of which are justified.

But we need not artificially heat up this competition as well. For it is not merely hilarious when a structurally erected impossibility is de-individualized by appeals to flexibility or increased work load from the individual. As when, on the one hand, the obligation, praised by all sides, is evoked, to prove one's »communication skills«; on the other hand, the omnipresent pressure to maintain confidentiality, to restrict information to small doses (»You shouldn't expect too much of the peasantry«), the tactical communication below a certain management level that people experience on the job. Frequently there is also the feeling of being completely cut off from the main lines of communication in the company.

It is anything but funny when the team premium is linked to down-sizing rates while everyone is practically compelled to repeat the old line of »job security as management task«. Nor is it merely amusing that only those improvement suggestions are eligible for premiums which apply to my colleague's responsibilities. Either I remain on my own turf, which means that any suggestion I might make is expected as part of my normal performance and, thus, is not eligible for a premium. Or, (the only way to get a premium) I poach on the turf of my team colleagues, the guy at the next desk, my partner or my boss, getting my premium and automatically turning the others into losers: »You missed that one, didn't you?« And that is the same colleague with whom I am supposed to work together closely in the »Quality 100« team.

Executives and employees experience this situation as nerve-jangling, over-demanding, conflictual. They sense that they cannot meet the contradictory demands, and frequently think of this as a personal failure. Wrongly. The solution is made structurally impossible. You have to get your feet on the ground to feel its shifting character.

Customer oriented – sales oriented

Remaining in a split position is painful. That is especially apparent if you take a look into the didactics of sales training sessions. The experts in this field have distanced themselves largely from the hard sell mentality of the past and now give people media-charged sessions in customer »consulting«, long-term customer »binding« and a professional analysis of customer needs during the sales discussion. Finally the salesperson is sent out with a »bonus-linked« assignment to get a certain number of product X out onto the market. Of course, he does that, since a major portion of his variable income is tied to it. The age-old guiding principle: »Cash consciousness works.«

In addition, the »how« question regarding sales in many companies is apparently highly dependent on business health: »customer-oriented« in good times. »Sales-oriented« in bad times. Sometimes quality is the focus, the salesperson acting as »consultant«, the customer's »confidant« who has detailed knowledge of internal company affairs. Sometimes he is expected to go back to »convincing« the customer, »get rid« of products, »get the stuff into circulation«. Frequently we get both messages simultaneously: »Total Customer Satisfaction«, on the one hand, and »Sell or be damned!« on the other.

Especially during a down turn the salespeople are told (confidentially) over and over again: »Be manipulative!« »Towards outsiders« we must add. For paradoxically the opposing message is »Be honest within the company!« The vocabulary of war towards outsiders – the vocabulary of peaceful cooperation to insiders. Right face! Left face! Dizziness can easily be the result. Finally, the dismay is complete if a salesperson turns the tables and applies manipulative techniques within the company. High trust culture!

The example of the salesperson clearly reveals the structure of the double-bind. People behave (in good times) as if »customer orientation« and »sales orientation« were *equivalent* values. But, in general, this is not at all true. Only if the customer orientation does *not* contradict the sales orientation does it remain a valid goal. Customer and sales orientation cannot always be reconciled. The sales orientation *includes*, so to speak, the customer orientation.

If both are situated in a *logical, hierarchical relationship* to each other (for example: customer orientation is a means to fulfill the purpose of sales orientation), then there is merely a situative decision-making problem. Double-binding (and confusing) is when

1. this value hierarchy is not marked
2. the chronological staggering (e.g. customer orientation now leads to rising sales *later*) remains unconsidered.

At this point a clarifying word is necessary. If one avoids making decisions one confuses the distinctly higher and lower ranking, nobody can differentiate between »intended« and »unintended«. Nothing remains then but a crash into depression.

Ruinous consequences

The double bind tears credibility to shreds. The understanding, mild analytical look which sees the realities and excuses the show because that's the way things just are, may be appropriate anywhere else but not when it comes to questions involving the survival of the company. But people who see through this show (and many do) distance themselves from it. For double-bind is a dishonest communication strategy towards those being addressed. It undermines the corporate culture from within. It pretends to provide goal-oriented practice when it really prevents it. Basically, it leads to nothing more than a loss of orientation and resignation.

That works – as is known and looked at cynically – on occasion, for a while. But the coat of paint covering the corruption of the company's policy is thin. When trust is needed, because a crisis looms, when loyalty is needed, in difficult times, when a »We can manage together!« is needed then the price falls due: »They're not going to tell me ...«

Donna Goya, Vice President Human Resources of Levi Strauss & Co., identifies one of the main dangers in achieving corporate goals as »mixed messages«. They cause corporate pathologies instead of creative cultures. From psychotherapy we know that double-binds can cause depressions. The bright and eager social energies which we so urgently need for creativity and innovation – where are they supposed to come from?

The scarcity of courage to make clear, authoritative value decisions leads to double-binds, inner conflicts, and missing favorable opportunities. The eternal marriage of on-the-one-hand and on-the-other brings forth consequences, firstly paralysis. Responsibility is not assumed, *cannot* be assumed. The paralyzing effect of this split and the feeling of not be able to meet contradictory demands, destroys any possible performance. *Nothing* is achieved, because everything should be achieved. This endangers the feeling of self-esteem. As a result, defense mechanisms are erected. People withdraw. Where once there was plenty, there is scarcity.

Tic-tac-toe

The double-bind show has apparent advantages. You can make demands – but you are not responsible. You are modern – but not accountable. You have committed yourself – and yet not really. Most importantly you can make someone else responsible. Depending on how you feel at the moment, you can re-evaluate. Especially when you have to produce the usual suspects: independent initiative becomes obstinacy, courage to take risks becomes recklessness, self-reliance becomes stubbornness. A demand always remains neglected, and can then be complained about. Similar to the game of tic-tac-toe, where, no matter which place the next X is marked, the O's win.

The double-bind immunizes the messenger against any appeal, thus supporting hierarchical power. For if there are no clear *overriding* yardsticks for required practice, everything depends on the current, capricious and arbitrary decision of the individual. Since such individuals do not commit themselves and do not comply to any generally valid yardsticks, their freedom of decision is unimpeded. The freedom of their employees is all the more restricted.

This inevitably creates the »please the boss« situation. The employees constantly keep an eye on the boss. People wonder whether the boss might perhaps twitch – then you can, as a preventative measure, twitch a little. Everybody looks upwards (instead of outwards: towards the customers). All the lines of energy lead to the boss. Moreover these bosses then complain that their employees do not take any responsibility and always wait for them to make a decision …

… the employees must also be hit over the head with a clothespin bag on occasion when they – without having to ask your prior approval – make any decisions. For that is the other side of the coin: employees notice the credibility gap, become cynical, remain passive, have inwardly already quit, and save their energy for their leisure time activities. It is an error to believe, the interests of hierarchy-oriented self-optimizers point in the same direction as the interests of the company. They optimize *themselves* but not the company; they take responsibility for *their* area, not for the whole; they invest in *their* careers, not in the performance potential of their employees. To put it quite frankly: A new contradiction is created de facto – between the individual interest of the hierarchically defined authority and the overall interest of the company.

Oral existing corporate cultures

I am not accusing anyone of bad intentions. But I can name at least three causes which also provide opportunities to escape from the crisis of conflicting messages.

1. In their corporate cultural feasibility lunacy many companies believed they could soften their really existing threadbare cultures by writing on glossy paper reams about focusing on people, or at least provide consolation by covering them with a smoke-screen. The top-down-missions which merely pretend to provide decisiveness and distinctly »clear relations«, trigger unrelated parallel double-binds. The impression is created that the immanent value messages are equally ranked. Especially the proclamation of this or that moral statement on corporate role models, leadership principles or the like creates the impression that the subject is one of eternal characteristics which must be displayed everywhere. The contradicting polarities – each of which has its justification – are announced with great sincerity in the direction of apparent clarity. They act as if there were no »other side«. The other pole is frequently even made taboo. They cover up the fact that there is a logical value hierarchy which orients itself towards the profitability of the company and individual power interests.

2. Very frequently the existing, oral corporate culture is denounced by concrete decisions. The practice caricaturizes the statement. For each company has a culture. It is the result of a long

growth process and is expressed in a certain manner of interaction. You cannot »introduce« a culture in the same way a new rule is introduced in football. In my experience the verbal messages in companies are completely unimportant. The only thing of importance – and which employees quickly pick up on – is the *unspoken* messages, as they become clear in concrete behavioral patterns, organizational structures and traditions. »You shall know them by their deeds« – wisely most people adhere to this Bible quote. *Deeds* are the real messages. These messages are clear. These messages are not subject to crises. That is why most CI brochures are so laughable. It is simply absurd to see how many heads of hierarchies dump their »visions« and »missions« on their employees, which contain values which did *not* contribute to the success of these managers in their careers.

3. The third cause lies somewhat deeper: every reference to values has the unpleasant consequence of discriminating against other values. But which of the messages should be given priority? Revealed truths are always in conflict with each other and each one insists on its morally supported claim to priority. But they cannot be spelled out in concrete moral practices since, if they were, they would come up against hard facts.

The decision on the agenda can be avoided if one clings to values which are meaningless. They are therefore easily forgotten because real life continues under the over-ambitious visions. Or one chooses bland phrases which sound radical. Then you have a lot to offer which automatically leaves the decision open. Or – thirdly – you refuse to choose. Choosing very often means deciding. That in turn means dropping another option, renunciation. The results are resistance, inner rebellion and passivity, if a choice is necessary.

But that, too, is just the surface level. For, in truth, one has chosen: indecision. But that also has advantages. One is afraid of responsibility – one refuses to take responsibility for the consequences of either/or decisions, especially for the option rejected. Just don't risk anything! The whole value discussion is a failure due to this lack of courage to clarity. What this produces is decorative terminology which does not commit people to anything but to its reproduction. Values are given a key position! To the right of the decimal point.

Guidelines? Sighed lines!

The double-bind is the method of superficially reconciling purpose and means while quietly picking out which one will be most profitable to you. That has disastrous consequences for the spiritual hygiene of the company, but especially for the credibility of the management. The paradox that it leaves behind is perhaps best illustrated by a short role game which was performed very successfully at a management symposium of an oil company by two managers: one manager is confronted after a long stay abroad with the new company guidelines:

»Who wrote this stuff, anyway?«

»Some ad agency or another. They probably just stole it from another company and switched the logos. And one of our task forces then adapted it a little bit, moved a couple of commas around. Finally it was approved by the directors.«

»Approved. Hummm. Just like that, no changes?«

»Oh yes ... They hired an attorney just to see to it that the wording is so general that nobody can hold them to it. Otherwise the thing would be a lot worse.«

»Look at this: ›Employees are primarily people.‹ Wow. The schedule of the Icelandic National Railway would be more informative. And this: ›We want to base our deeds on the principles of a socially responsible market economy.‹ That is intended to make us think, right? ›XY Inc. (no, I won't reveal the company) is striving for progress.‹ Well, how about that, now! ›We make a serious effort to support fair competition.‹ Whenever I think of all the serious *efforts* I have already made… ›We respect recognized, ethical standards.‹ Is it time to applaud yet?«

»Has anyone actually looked into whether these statements mesh with the other policies, implementing regulations and leadership instruments?«

»Is that important?«

»There might be a few nasty contradictions.«

»You're nitpicking. Nobody notices things like that!«

»Did you at least adapt the leadership seminars to the new principles?«

»Come off it. The principles are so general you can read anything into them. They have about as much orientation value as a magnetic compass on the North Pole. We don't have to change anything.«

»How did the employees react?«

»They laughed their heads off.«

»Why?«

»They didn't realize it had to do with their company. ›Must have been sent to the wrong address‹ they said.«

In the USA this type of business ethics is confined to the area where it belongs: marketing. Such guidelines say everything and, therefore, nothing. A functional morality contains clear value decisions, correspondingly also decisions *against* alternative value concepts. This decision must be made and may not dissipate into a not-only-but-also.

The country needs new values!

Objection: *but people need some kind of orientation!* The irony is that it is precisely the dissonance between the conflicting top-down revelations which in effect means moral relativism. One example: If we had not promoted our corporate culture so much our fall in 1992/94 would not have been so dramatic. But the way things are, all the talk about »dialogue« and »focus on people« has been exposed as corporate cultural stuffing. New German Euphemistics: Formerly we wrote that so and so many people would be made redundant, now companies are »slimming down«. Sounds nicer, somehow. We successfully managed companies even in the days of corporate identity. Precisely *because* the corporate messages are blared all over, there arises the opportunity of comparing deeds and words, which otherwise would not be exposed, or at least not so completely. If I announce messages, I have to live them. But then I do not have to announce them anymore.

Is there nothing left for us among the ruins of transparency except laughter as a final consolation? Laughing as a corrective reaction to corporate cultural real-life satire? Even if some things are no longer funny but simply laughable, there is still something which can be done:

1. Any double-bind is to be resolved. You have to drop one guideline where concurrence was previously the rule. These reference systems and yardsticks must be capable of providing orientation and serve as a solid basis for demands. To this end it is helpful to develop them together. If these reference systems are set up in dialogue, people will also take responsibility for them.

2. We need transparency in the value hierarchy. The reference systems must be positioned in a logical, hierarchical relationship to each other. We must not put together a hodge-podge of values and make believe that they are equivalent. If you can only follow messages by *not* following them, what is left is confusion and people who look to the »top« for decisions to be made. That is the end of commitment in the company.

3. What makes leadership so difficult is to require: the readiness to recognize conflicts of principle and to assume the necessary »carefully considered« or »creative« responsibility. To face the dilemma of conflicting interests, to present the conflict openly and completely, to indicate the consequences and – to make a

choice available. Not to pretend the whole situation were clear and free of tension. This requires managers who open their eyes to values and interests, which are both justified and, therefore, need to be balanced against each other over and over.

4. When you are dealing with processes of change have the courage to consign some things to the attic, to disassociate yourself from things which have outlived their relevance … If – as so often – more and more is added, the confusion has to increase.

5. Heinrich Heine wrote in his cycle of poems »Germany, a Winter's Tale«: »I am familiar with the style, I am familiar with the text, I am familiar with the men who wrote it; I know, they drink wine behind closed doors, and publicly preach in favor of water.« What we need are managers who are credible. Who live what they proclaim, and do not stage public »as if« events and do the opposite later.

Credibility

»Every consequence bears resistance within it« – this central thought in Martin Heidegger's Freiburger rectorate's speech indicates how precarious and sensitive the task of leadership is. Without mutual trust, without an organic relationship between managers and employees this task cannot be achieved. Yet, in recent years we have seen more erosion of employee trust in management than ever before. According to the statements of many older managers, in the post-war years, there has never been a similar credibility gap between top management and employees as there is today. (Certainly exasperated by the immense income differences between those on top and those at the bottom which stigmatize some appeals to economize.)

Many companies believe power oriented self-optimizers among the managers fulfill company interests better. That is why key positions are often occupied by power-oriented people. The social tactics they choose are always on the right side, and being unaffected, are quite satisfied. »When I convince them that, from today, ›cooperative‹ is the better way, then it will work better.« In this context leadership and power are often confused: They say »Our issue is leadership« but they mean »Our issue is power«. To them, power means *power over others*, not *power to accomplish*.

From what has been said up till now, personality characteristics emerge which can be considered requirements for credible leadership. In part I have in mind the thoughts Peter Runderle expressed in »Liberal Integrity«.

1) Words must match deeds.

»Walk the talk«: This is *outward* harmony. A commitment culture is only possible if words and deeds do not contradict each other. To emphasize this again: this credibility as a form is indifferent to any moral substance. It is not a question of »right« or »wrong« values, not a question of truth. But of truthfulness. To this end it is also important to reject the feelings of the moment which result from old patterns, and to submit to a self-obligated standard. The British say: »Put your money where your mouth is.«

Every manager type, who I would refer to as *sentimental dreamer*, sidesteps this condition. They are full of good will, but they do not want to pay the price for decisive action. They do not want to choose. They announce. That is free. But they do not act correspondingly. For then they would have to reckon with disadvantages. They have convictions, but they do not stand up for them. They content themselves with the feeling of analyzing matters, intellectually cushioned and morally superior, when they reason about what should be done or not done. But this thinking is a substitute for action. They lay back in the awareness that they know what *should* be done. Their primary interest is the favorable opinion which they have of themselves and which others have of them.

Very frequently they turn any tensions which may arise from this outwards, by rigidly demanding that *others* accept the consequences. Do something themselves? Then a price would have to be paid. Self-delusion as a personal principle. Their deeds say that their words are lies. »Did I promised that? I must have chosen my words poorly.«

The sentimental dreamers cannot assume responsibility for themselves nor for the lives of other people. Their resigned fatalism justifies irresponsible inaction. Important is: This – very common – type of manager is not capable of making agreements. Obligation and binding agreements are foreign to them. They cannot facilitate a culture based on commitment. But they have a guilty conscience, and that is the guarantee that their behavior will remain steady. Being sophisticated, they »trade in« their guilty conscience, so to speak, in order to keep themselves inwardly in balance. This trick allows them to leave everything the way it is.

2) Value must be a goal in itself.

The basic condition for credibility states that a proclaimed value is lived for its own sake and not for the sake of another, hidden value. Genuine credibility is not calculating. This is the condition of *inner* harmony. To give an example, such a credible manager protects the environment because it is important to protect the environment, and not to look better in the eyes of critical public opinion. But anyone who, for example, addresses their employees in a friendly manner, not to be friendly, but to be able to manipulate them better, does not meet this condition. This equally applies to those who join the trend towards dismantling hierarchies not because it is sensible for the purposes specified but because they want to appear up to date.

In the typology of dubiousness it is the *corrupt usefulness calculator* who fails. They act in conformance with their words but to achieve another goal. Their line of approach is exclusively directed towards obtaining personal advantages. For these they will pay any price. Being opportunistic and cynical they have no convictions. Their behavior is not colored by any inward depth. Their passions are wealth and power.

This manager type is not capable of making agreements either; they break any obligation for the sake of personal advantage. If this is threatened, commitment means nothing to them. They are better off: in contrast to the sentimental dreamer, they have no feelings of guilt. The voice of their conscience never fully reaches maturity.

3) Values must be capable of revision.

Credible managers do not simply live their values, they give reasons for them as well. They expose their values to a general review. They are ready and able to discuss their values – to question them and, if necessary to revise them. That means in particular, to re-evaluate repeatedly the consequences of those values for the future of others and oneself and – if no acceptable reason can be justified – to revise them.

The *fundamentalist fanatic* – a generally rare manager type – will not want to fulfill this credibility condition. Their practice matches their words but they are hardly prepared to justify their selections of values or to revise them. They would love to raise their conviction to a general standard of practice, even at the price of forcing others to comply.

The condition of credibility

In the relationship between managers and employees power lies in the hands of the latter. Employees are management's customers. Employees choose their leadership with their energy and commitment. If anyone is empowered at all, then it is the employees who empower their managers. Not the other way around. But under what conditions are people recognized as leaders? Not thanks to their hierarchical position. Fear, status and money do not generate commitment. They generate conformism and adherence to standards.

Credibility makes the difference. Credibility is the absolute prerequisite for leadership in a commitment culture. It defines the quality of the relationship between partners.

If the principle of commitment is the central formative idea in the company, then you are only credible as a manager under one condition: if you want to be credible, not because it is morally good or because it is applauded by others. But because you have chosen it. For no other reason.

Epilogue

On February 3rd, 1965, the radio station Free Berlin transmitted a debate between the two philosophers Theodor W. Adorno and Arnold Gehlen. But the dispute, so sensitively recorded by Hauke Brunkhorst, did not initially get off the ground. It was not until the subject of individual responsibility came up, the ability of each individual to reflect, that the gulf between the two, joining and separating them simultaneously, became visible. Gehlen assumes, along with Aristotle, that there are never more than a *few* people who are capable of acting reflectively and responsibly, but the *majority* would collapse under the weight of responsibility. For him, the crisis symptoms of modern times are due to *too much* reflection. We need, therefore, strong and authoritarian institutions which relieve people of responsibility, i. e. which treat them to a certain extent as incapable.

Adorno was completely different. For him it is precisely the authoritarian institutions which inhibit self-actualization and, correspondingly, the development of the individual's capacities as well. He agrees with Descartes' and Kant's assumption that the ability to act responsibly is the »best distributed thing in the world« and that all people are endowed with the *potential* to reflect. Therefore, conditions must be created which permit this potential to be actualized. In response to Gehlen's question whether one should really expect *everyone* to be responsible, Adorno said: »I can only answer that with one word: Yes! … I believe that people, as long as they are over-protected (by authoritarian institutions in the sense of Gehlens – R. S.) and are not granted full responsibility and self-determination, that their happiness in this world will also remain a mere chimera.« Gehlen: »We've touched precisely the point at which you say ›yes‹ and I say ›no‹.«

According to Gehlen we cannot get beyond obligation as mere service in the form of conformism and subordination. Adorno says, there is a real chance to assume individual responsibility, to be committed, to actualize one's own abilities as the potential of freedom.

We can choose.

A word of thanks

What I had to say is nothing new. In fact, it is quite old. At least 2 to 3 thousand years old. Much of this you were already familiar with. Perhaps you had forgotten some of this knowledge; perhaps in some cases I have pushed open a door a little more which had already been somewhat ajar. Often, when I felt doubtful, I remembered a statement made by Ludwig Wittgenstein from his early days at university: »... what I have written here, does not claim in detail to be anything new ..., because I am unconcerned about whether something which I thought had already been thought of by someone else before me.« This statement made a strong impression on me at the time, and I would like to add: For me it was new when I thought of it, when I had a great deal of satisfaction putting it together again.

Yet I would still like to mention those who have contributed. For nobody writes a book alone. The list of names of those from whom I learned a great deal would be nearly as long as the book itself. Primarily: Fichte, Heidegger, Kant, Nietzsche, and Popper are the watermarks of this paper, whose influence have left a mark on my writing. So: (almost) everything is just filched. The patient and intelligent cheerfulness of Ralph Waldo Emerson – the personification of America's spiritual declaration of independence – I owe more than I could express here. His relevance never ceases to surprise me.

The trains of thought contained in this book are thus not merely the property of the author but belong to a certain intellectual atmosphere which an individual can neither generate nor encompass. Traces were left by my friend Peter Ricken, Marianne Hammann, Brigitte Roser, Marieluise Wiemer, Karl-Bernd Greve, Michael Irle, Dieter Lange and Christ Quiske from IAK Burscheid, Franz Lux, Fritz B. Simon, Klaus M. Wilsmann as well as Peter Weiss from Recursos, Santa Fe, New Mexico.

But I would like to thank primarily all the many people in the companies who have helped me grow with their questions and problems. They all had something to teach me: People who are only familiar with management theory, are not familiar with anything.